Sporting LEGENDS

GEORGE BEST
⌐ HIS GREATEST MATCHES ↄ

PUBLISHED BY
Anthem Publishing Ltd
Suite 6, Piccadilly House,
London Road, Bath BA1 6PL
Tel +44 (0) 1225 489984
Fax +44 (0) 1225 489980

EDITOR
Jon Palmer
jon.palmer@anthem-publishing.com

SENIOR ART EDITOR
Jenny Cook
jenny.cook@anthem-publishing.com

EDITORIAL DIRECTOR
Paul Pettengale
paul.pettengale@anthem-publishing.com

ADVERTISING DIRECTOR
Simon Lewis
simon.lewis@anthem-publishing.com

PUBLISHING DIRECTOR
Jon Bickley
jon.bickley@anthem-publishing.com

PHOTOGRAPHY
Pictures © Empics unless otherwise credited
www.empics.co.uk

PRINT
Garnett Dickinson
Tel +44 (0) 1709 364721

OVERSEAS DISTRIBUTION
Marketforce (UK) Ltd,
5th Floor, Low Rise Building,
King's Reach Tower, Stamford Street,
London SE1 9LS
Tel +44 (0) 20 7633 3300

UK DISTRIBUTION
Anthem Publishing

LICENSING ENQUIRIES
Jon Bickley
jon.bickley@anthem-publishing.com

Anthem
PUBLISHING

ISBN 0-9552170-0-8

When we were planning to feature
George Best as our first subject in
this series of Sporting Legends, we
hoped this tribute would serve to
commemorate his 60th birthday,
which would have fallen in May. Sadly, it wasn't to
be. George died on 25 November last year, at the
frighteningly young age of 59.

Right up until the very end, I always thought
he'd somehow pull through, like he always did.
You kind of expected it of him. We all knew he
was ill; he'd been ill for several years, but he'd
always come through. It was like when you
thought he'd tried to go past one defender too
many; that he should have passed to a team mate
but he hadn't, and now he'd lost possession. And
then, inexplicably, he'd come out of the tackle
with the ball still at his feet.

We all identified with the outpouring of grief
that surrounded his funeral in Belfast. So many
people have so many happy memories – even those
too young to ever see him play. And now we want
to remember his football. There were times when
what went on off the pitch was inextricably linked
to what happened on it, and we've talked about
that, but this isn't a tale of drinking, womanising
and gambling. That's none of our business. This is
a story about football. And in particular, about
one man who played the game very well.

Was he the greatest ever? Does it matter? Pelé
said he was, and that was good enough for George.
But for what it's worth, I'm with Jimmy Greaves
on this: it's a silly question. But there was never
anyone better than George. *Sporting* LEGENDS

Jon Palmer

CONTENTS

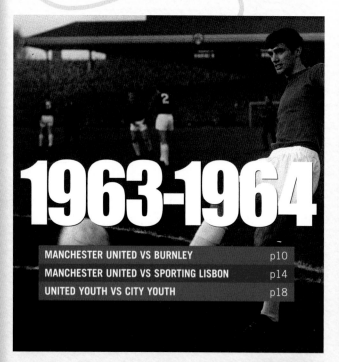

1963-1964

1964-1965

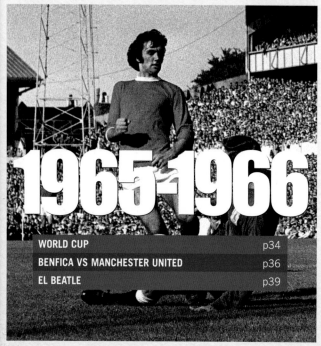

1965-1966

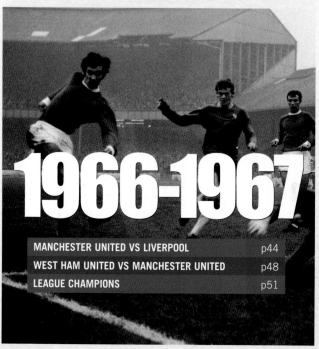

1966-1967

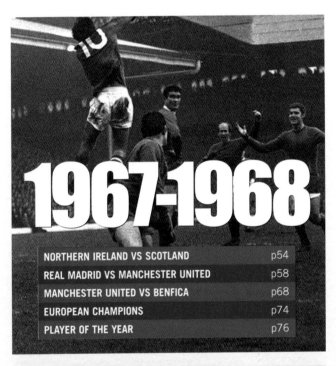

1967-1968

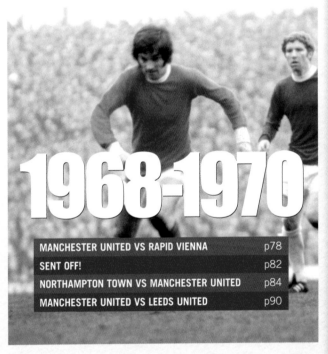

1968-1970

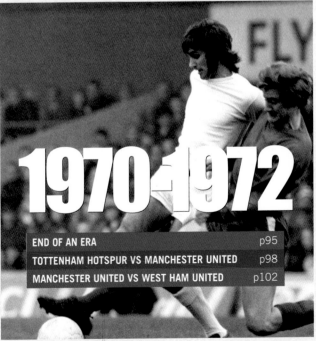

1970-1972

1972-1988

BELFAST BOY

"We never had trouble finding him. If you wanted him, you looked in the field at the end of the road, or by the garages, and he'd be there with a ball." **Dickie Best**

As soon as he started to walk, there were inklings around the Cregagh Estate that Dickie and Ann Best's baby boy had something of a yen for the game of football: he was kicking a ball as an infant and taking one to bed with him as a toddler. He'd lie in bed and cuddle it, saying, "One day, you'll do everything I tell you to do." When he went to school he played football every lunchtime and after school every night. He would often play on well after dark, on his own if he had to, until a family member came to collect him.

In the winter he used to come home, his skinny legs trembling from the cold in his

George Best came from good sporting stock: his father, Dickie, played amateur football to a good standard…

…while his mother was an international standard hockey player. Ann, tragically, dealt with her son's fame no better than he did. Teetotal until the age of 40, she drank herself to death by the age of 54.

short trousers and his laces frozen solid, and so muddy that he had to be hosed down outside before he could be let in for a hot bath. But every night he'd stay out to play football. And if there wasn't a football he'd play with a tennis ball. He'd try to kick the tennis ball against the knob on the garage door. If he didn't kick it right, the ball would bounce back at any angle; the trick was to hit the doorknob straight on, so the ball would bounce straight back to him. A tennis ball. And when he could do that properly he'd start working on his left foot.

THE RUSSIANS ARE COMING

Geordie, as he's always been known in Belfast, began to follow Wolverhampton Wanderers and keep a scrapbook of their exploits. Wolves were one of the most successful teams in England in the 1950s and the first British club to play in Europe – in friendlies arranged against the likes of Honved, Spartak Moscow and Dinamo Moscow; curious, alien foreigners, some of whom had recently started showing the British how to really play the game – and sometimes the matches were shown on the telly.

Mr Harrison had a telly and the ritual was that George would kick a ball against the wall of his house until Mr Harrison stepped out and invited him in to watch the match. George's grandfather, who was also called George, used to take his grandson to see Glentoran from time to time, but the boy generally preferred to be playing football rather than watching it. Wolves, however, did capture his imagination. He knew they played in gold, though it could have been any colour on Mr Harrison's tiny black-and-white television. But this was the club the boy was always playing for whenever he was dreaming of scoring winning goals in the FA Cup final.

Getting noticed

AS GEORGE'S REPUTATION spread across Belfast, scouts would appear on the touchlines whenever George played in organised matches. But, although the boy could obviously play, he was always rejected for being too small and skinny. Then, when he was 15, Bud McFarlane, the manager of Cregagh Boys Club, persuaded Bob Bishop to come to watch his star player.

Bishop was Manchester United's chief scout in Northern Ireland. He was also very well connected in the province and was responsible for the Boyland Youth Club side, an under-18 team with a growing reputation for supplying United with young talent. Bishop was persuaded to invite George to train with Boyland, and was sufficiently impressed with what he saw to arrange a match between Cregagh and Boyland – 15-year-olds against 17- and 18-year-olds – just to see if the lad could cut it with the bigger boys, or whether he really was too small to make it as a professional.

Cregagh won 4-2 and Best scored twice. That was enough. Bishop, a man who had quite a reputation for understatement in his appraisals, immediately fired off a telegram to Matt Busby: "I think I've found you a genius."

➤ ELEVEN-PLUS

When he passed his eleven-plus exam, the only kid in his class to do so, George was sent to grammar school, which involved a trip across a predominantly Catholic area, in his Protestant school blazer. The taunts he endured as he ran that gauntlet were nothing compared to what would happen when the Troubles started; nothing to compare with the death in 1974 of his cousin Gary Reid, who was killed by a bullet when he was caught in crossfire on his way to the fish and chip shop. But it was enough to start George skipping school. This gave him yet more time to practise his football, while his schoolwork deteriorated. He later went back to join his friends at the local secondary school, but George now also recognises that his truancy was not dissimilar to the way he would later disappear when something went wrong in his life, or looked like it might.

The Cregagh Estate of George's youth had no graffiti, no one locked their doors and Protestants and Catholics lived side by side with never more than a bit of name-calling. In 1990, George wrote that he now saw the place as "grey and soulless" but added that he still had to remind his dad to lock the door when he went out. Dickie later retorted that if George thought it was still like that in Belfast, he'd been away too long.

THIRTY-A-SIDE

George was a shy child and never very sure of himself; he was never even fully confident of his footballing abilities and always worked diligently to improve them. But when he was a lad on the Cregagh Estate, even the older boys couldn't get the ball off him.

He'd play in games that began with just him kicking his tennis ball up against a wall until someone else came along. Then they'd play one-on-one, then two-on-two, right up to twenty- or thirty-a-side. As the games went on it became more and more difficult to keep the ball, because there were more meddling feet and less space to play in. But keep the ball he did. He considered it an affront if anyone took it off him, even the older boys. And he was still barely five foot and seven stone when Bob Bishop invited him to Old Trafford at the age of fifteen. *Sporting* LEGENDS

> *"From day one, all I ever wanted to do was play football, and that's all I did."* **George Best**

Eric McMordie
(Middlesbrough)

George and Eric's Bogus Journey

ONE HOT JULY DAY IN 1961, a boy called Eric McMordie turned up at the Best house with his bags packed ready for a two-week trial at Old Trafford. With only expense money for assistance, the pair intrepidly negotiated the prescribed trip to Manchester – neither had ever been further than Bangor before – and, when nobody came to meet them at the station, they sensibly decided to catch a taxi to the ground. It all seemed to be going very well, until the taxi driver asked: "Which Old Trafford?" The boys had never heard of the cricket ground.

Manchester United didn't go to great lengths to welcome triallists, even one as eagerly anticipated as George Best, and the mere sight of Harry Gregg, the first team's man-mountain of a goalkeeper, struck fear into the heart. The boys also met Matt Busby, another awe-inspiring experience that only served to hasten the spiral of their homesickness. Within two days they had agreed that Manchester was not for them.

On the boat back home, George dejectedly told his new friend that he didn't think he was good enough to play professional football. Eric replied that he thought he did have what it took, but that he wanted to play in a nice town, by the sea.

Unsurprisingly, this wasn't the first time a triallist had gone missing and Matt Busby soon wrote to Dickie Best to say that George would be welcome back any time. "Maybe at Christmas," Dickie told his son. "No, I want to go now," George replied. He went, and within two years he would be on the verge of the first team. Eric's dream also came true, in a way: he went on to have a successful career with Middlesbrough.

1963-1964

After just two years at the club, George is promoted to the Manchester United first team for the 1963/64 season. He is still only 17 years old and still eligible to play for the youth team.

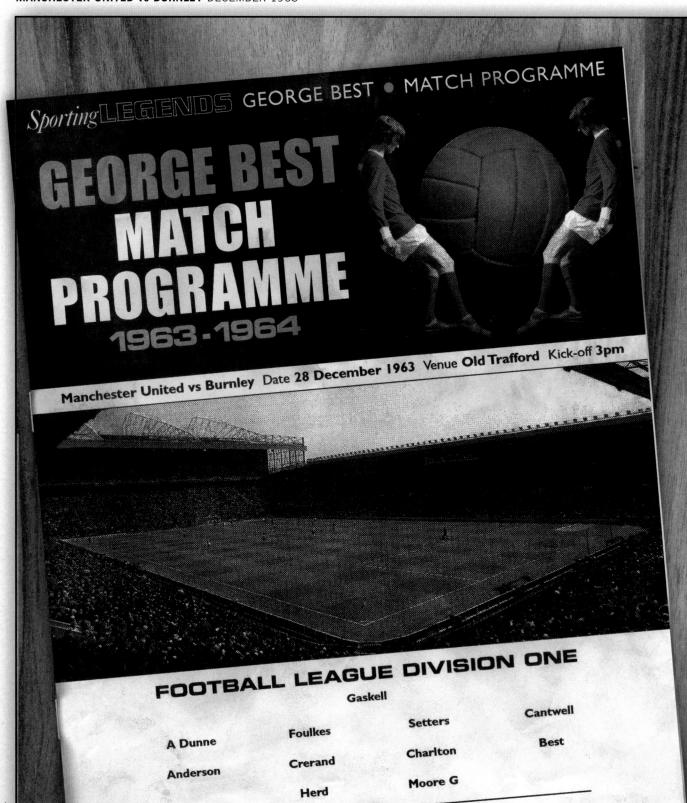

❧ FOOTBALL LEAGUE DIVISION ONE ❧

Manchester United

VS

Burnley

VENUE	Old Trafford
DATE	Saturday, 28 December 1963
KICK-OFF	3pm

Five years had passed since the Munich air crash and now a new generation of young players was beginning rise through the Old Trafford ranks. Johnny Giles left for Leeds United in the summer after trying to tell Matt Busby how to run his football team. Dave Sadler stepped in for David Herd, and while neither of them would ever quite make the grade, both Ian Moir and Phil Chisnall were given their chance to prove themselves.

But George would get his turn soon enough. After only three reserve matches he was named 12th man (there were no substitutes in those days) for the game against West Bromwich Albion on 14 September. He still wouldn't normally have played, but Ian Moir pulled out injured at the last moment. Paddy Crerand knew that George would be playing and told him so as the team got on the bus, but George didn't believe it until Matt Busby wandered down the aisle and spoke to him as he went past: "You're in today, son."

"YOU DID FINE, SON"

George did enough on his debut to earn him a "You did fine, son" from the boss and some kind words from his team-mates in the bath after the game. There was even a "Boy Best flashes in Red

After two successive defeats in which they had conceded ten goals (six to Burnley and four to Everton) Matt Busby decided it was time to end the season of goodwill. For the return fixture against Burnley he brought in two young wingers, Willie Anderson and George Best – to much criticism from the press, who were generally of the opinion that you wouldn't win anything with kids.

attack" headline in the *Manchester Evening News*, above a report that spoke well of "the prospect of young George Best to brighten a dullish match".

Despite the praise, George knew he hadn't done enough to keep his place in the team. By Christmas he still hadn't been recalled and he returned to Belfast to spend the holidays with his family, as he always had done. But on Boxing Day, United were beaten 6-1 at Turf Moor. The day after Boxing Day, the telegram boy picked his path, amid much commotion, up Burren Way to the Best house.

"If it's important enough for them to send a telegram, you must be playing," said his father. But George didn't want to leave his family at Christmas if he wasn't sure he was going to play, so he telephoned the club to say that if he went back, they would have to fly him back home to Belfast immediately after the match. It was agreed, which made his father even more convinced that his son was going to play. The next day, as George set off for Manchester, Dickie spoke to the club trainer, Jack Crompton, who confirmed his hopes.

➤

👁 EYEWITNESS **What the players said...**

"Their left back was a good player, Alex Elder, but George destroyed him, absolutely murdered him." **Pat Crerand**

THE OPPOSITION

THE BURNLEY team that won the League in 1960 was getting old. They had finished as runners-up to Alf Ramsey's Ipswich Town in 1962, also reaching the FA

Cup final that season, but this was undoubtedly a side on the wane. Never the less, Burnley had won 6-1 at Turf Moor on Boxing Day and Matt Busby had judged that he

Alex Elder

would need to change his wingers for the return fixture two days later. In came the 16-year-old Willie Anderson on the left, and the 17-year-old George Best on the right.

Up against the teenagers was the defensive partnership of Alex Elder and John Angus. It would prove a torrid afternoon for both full backs.

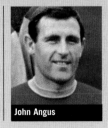
John Angus

After this performance, Matt Busby just couldn't leave the young Irishman out of the side.

© Colorsport

OFF THE PITCH Number 1
28 December 1963

The Beatles
I Want To Hold Your Hand
Dominique
The Singing Nun

"Their left back was a good player, Alex Elder, but George destroyed him, absolutely murdered him. So much so that I actually felt sorry for Alex. George ran him silly for the whole game. It wasn't just the odd occasion, like it had been with [West Brom's] Graham Williams, this was total annihilation. George was magnificent."

PANG OF SYMPATHY

John Angus got done a couple of times too. Angus was a friend of Bobby Charlton, who remembers how his pal, an England international himself, was turned inside out by George Best. Like Crerand, Charlton also felt sympathy for an opposition full back as Best knocked the ball through his legs: "Angus set off in the direction he thought George would go in, but he never did."

EYEWITNESS What the papers said...

"Willie Anderson, 16, and George Best, 17, who was having his second game, were a pair of wingers who gave the experienced Angus and Elder quite an afternoon. Best got himself on the scoresheet to complete a mature display."

News of the World

➤ "Yes, Mr Best, he's playing all right."

"If I'd known that, I'd have come over with him," Dick replied.

"Don't worry, Mr Best," said Crompton. "There'll be many more games."

TOTAL ANNIHILATION

George was up against Burnley left back Alex Elder, who had already established himself as a first choice for Northern Ireland. George has described walking out onto the pitch that day. "The tunnel at Old Trafford is on a slope and as you walk down you can see the crowd opening out in front of you. When the first spectators see you they start to cheer and the noise spreads around the whole stadium in an instant, getting louder and louder. I can still recall the way the hairs on the back of my neck stood up."

Pat Crerand describes what happened next:

DID YOU KNOW?
Alex Elder and George Best would later become team mates for Northern Ireland. Elder won 40 caps; Best 37.

George capped a fine performance by scoring with a right-footed shot from the edge of the area. And, just as the club had promised, he was back at home in Belfast that night to celebrate New Year. The next day all the talk in Cregagh was about what was they'd seen in the *Belfast Telegraph*. The paper had already carried a local-boy-made-good piece after his debut against West Brom, but this time there was a picture of the Best boy on the back page, scoring for Manchester United. *Sporting*LEGENDS

THE RESULT	
MANCHESTER UNITED	**BURNLEY**
Herd (2), **5**	**1**
Moore G (2), Best	Lochhead

ATTENDANCE 54,000

BE A PART OF IT

IFA OFFICIAL SUPPORTERS SCHEME

join online at www.irishfa.com

The IFA - Bringing Communities Together

Sporting LEGENDS GEORGE BEST • MATCH PROGRAMME

GEORGE BEST MATCH PROGRAMME
1963 · 1964

Manchester United vs Sporting Lisbon Date **26 February 1964** Venue **Old Trafford** Kick-off **8pm**

ECWC QUARTER FINAL FIRST LEG

Gaskell

Setters   A Dunne

Foulkes

Brennan   Stiles   Best

Charlton

Crerand   Herd

Law

Osvaldo

Figuetredo   Geo

Mendes

Morais   Alfredo   Gomes

Baptista

Hilario   Carlos

Carvalho

ECWC QUARTER FINAL FIRST LEG
Manchester United
VS
Sporting Lisbon

VENUE	Old Trafford
DATE	Wednesday, 26 February 1964
KICK-OFF	8pm

Ten short weeks before this European Cup Winners Cup match, back before Christmas, on the night of 10 December to be precise, George had been just one of 50,000 people watching from the Old Trafford stands as Manchester United played Tottenham Hotspur in the second round of the same competition. The opponents that night may have been English, but they were still the holders of the trophy and the atmosphere was like any European game.

George later recalled that it felt like the Wolves games he used to watch on the telly in Belfast, only this time he was there in the crowd to cheer as the teams came running out onto the pitch under the baleful glow of the floodlights.

ENIGMATIC WINGER
Tottenham held a 2-0 lead from the first leg at White Hart Lane and few people gave Manchester United much of a chance of overcoming the deficit. As well as their star players Dave Mackay and Jimmy Greaves, the Lillywhites also had the enigmatic winger Cliff Jones. Like George himself, Jones could go past defenders at will, but didn't always look for the easy pass. "The ball is round," his manager Bill Nicholson had often

Manchester United come into the game on the back of two good League wins in local derbies. They have just beaten Blackburn Rovers 3-1 away following a 5-0 home win over Bolton Wanderers. They have also just progressed to the 6th round of the FA Cup with a 4-0 win over Barnsley.

pleaded with the Welshman. "Why don't you pass it sometimes?"

But Jones or no Jones, that night wasn't going to be Tottenham's night – Bobby Charlton and David Herd both scored twice as United caused a major upset by beating the 1961 domestic double winners 4-1 on the night and 4-3 on aggregate. It was an impressive result and a great game for the United supporters, and Matt Busby, who had just caught a glimpse of a piece of European silverware that would sit nicely in the trophy room while he continued to work on his plan to achieve his ultimate goal, the European Cup.

EUROPEAN DEBUT
As George left the Spurs game that night with the rest of the crowd, he too may have imagined himself amid such glory as his memories of ➤

👁 EYEWITNESS **What the players said...**

"I can only remember George in the first team. He all but missed the reserves, going straight from the youth team to the firsts. He was on top of us before we knew what had happened." **Bobby Charlton**

THE OPPOSITION

THOUGH IT WAS now Benfica who were the dominant force in Portuguese football, and indeed European football, Sporting Lisbon came to Manchester in good form.

Having knocked out Atalanta in the first round, the 1962 Portuguese champions gave Apoel Nicosia something of a mountain to climb in the second leg of

Carvalho

the second round by beating them 16-1 in Lisbon. Sporting were a resilient side who played in green and white hoops, like Glasgow Celtic, and despite the result of

this match at Old Trafford, it would eventually be they, not Manchester United, who would join the Scottish Cup holders in the semi final of the Cup Winners Cup.

Hilario

Manchester United's
Denis Law (centre)
scores the opening goal
in his team's 4-1 win.

➤ watching Wolves on Mr Harrison's telly back in Belfast now mingled with the sights and sounds he had just witnessed close up. But by this time he had only played one game for the first team. How much would he have believed that he would actually be playing in the next round of the European Cup Winners Cup?

Manchester United were drawn to play Sporting Clube de Portugal in the quarter final, with the first leg at Old Trafford. By now, Best was fast staking a claim for a regular place in the first team and the match against the 1962 Portuguese champions was just one of a series of debuts that came thick and fast. The week after the Burnley game, both he and Willie Anderson were retained for the FA Cup third round encounter at the Dell, which United won 3-2. And on the 15th of April, after barely 20 games for United, he would make his Northern Ireland debut against Wales in Swansea. Come the end of the calendar year he would have scored for Manchester United in a European club game and also for his country, and it wouldn't be long before he was scoring regularly for both teams.

THE LAWMAN

For now, though, Denis Law was the leading man, as he showed against Sporting. This hat trick was Law's second in the competition that season – he had already scored one against Willem II Tilburg in the first round. And his star was not about to fade. In a remarkable series of achievements, Law scored another hat trick against Djurgaarden in the Inter City Fairs Cup the following season; that

one coming in a 6-1 win in which Best also scored, the first of his 11 European goals.

But there would be a disastrous end to this season's European campaign. In the return leg in Portugal on March 18, it was Osvaldo Silva's turn to score a hat trick as Sporting romped to a 5-0 victory, with all five goals coming in the first 60 minutes. United were knocked out of the Cup in just as much style as they had shown in disposing of the holders in December. After that match in Lisbon, Matt Busby, who rarely said much after a game, tore into his players. This wasn't the European Cup he yearned for, but it was the Cup Winners Cup and his men had let him down with an abject performance. George remembers that they were "absolutely terrible" that night. "Our worst ever performance in Europe," was how he rated it at the end of his career.

Sporting went on to win the European Cup Winners Cup that year, but it got worse than that. Manchester United were knocked out of the FA Cup at the semi final stage by eventual winners West Ham and Busby had to console himself with a League runners up spot behind Bill Shankly's fast-emerging Liverpool. *Sporting* LEGENDS

THE RESULT

MANCHESTER UNITED	SPORTING LISBON	
4	**1**	ATTENDANCE
Law (3), Charlton	Osvaldo	60,000

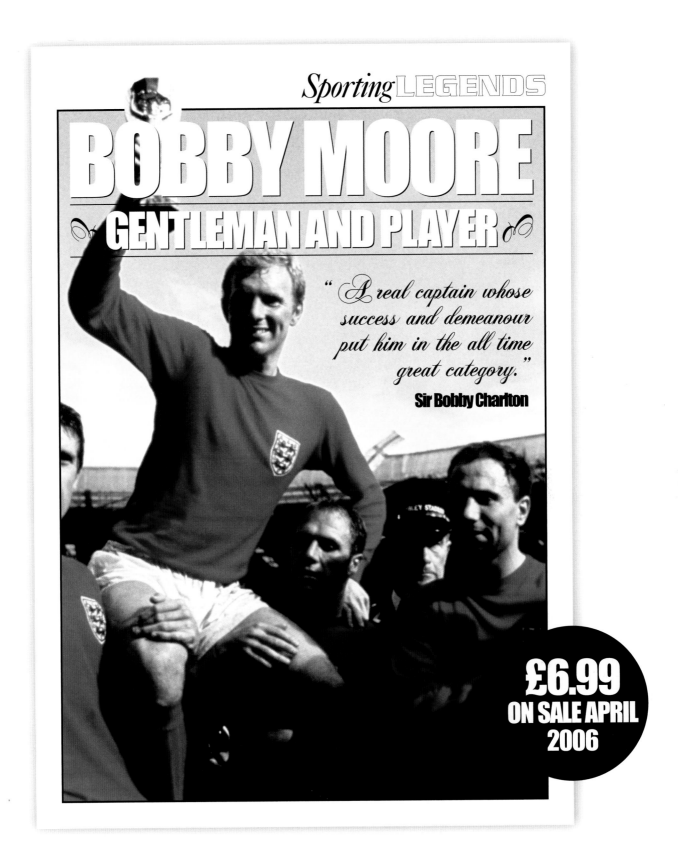

An affectionate tribute to England's greatest
ever captain marking the 40th anniversary
of the nation's World Cup triumph.

Sporting**LEGENDS** GEORGE BEST ● MATCH PROGRAMME

GEORGE BEST MATCH PROGRAMME
1963-1964

Manchester United vs Manchester City Date **8 April 1964** Venue **Old Trafford** Kick-off **7.30pm**

FA YOUTH CUP SEMI FINAL FIRST LEG

Rimmer

Noble

Duff

Fitzpatrick

Farrar

McBride

Kinsey   Anderson

Sadler

Aston   Best

●

Pardoe   Frost

Jones

Connor   McAlinden

Clay

Wood

Burrows

Doyle

Wild

Ogley

FA YOUTH CUP SEMI FINAL FIRST LEG
Manchester United
VS
Manchester City

VENUE	Old Trafford
DATE	Wednesday, 8 April 1964
KICK-OFF	7.30pm

Any match between United and City has always been a big game in Manchester, but this FA Youth Cup semi final encounter carried an extra significance: the previous season, as Manchester United set about winning the FA Cup, Manchester City had been relegated – by their local rivals.

When the two clubs had met in the spring of 1963, with both perilously close to relegation, Denis Law had won a contentious penalty six minutes from time, which Albert Quixall had converted to earn United the point they needed to be sure of avoiding the drop, and which sent City to Upton Park needing a result. The Blues were beaten 6-1 by West Ham and relegated.

This meant that for the first time since 1949 there would be no Manchester derby. And by April 1964 it had become apparent that there wasn't going to be one next season either – despite the goals of Derek Kevan and Jimmy Murray, Manchester City were not good enough to bounce straight back from the Second Division. In 1964, the FA Youth Cup was the only hope of glory for the blue half of the city.

None would ever quite achieve the success of George Best but no fewer than 17 of the boys who played in this game went on to play for their first teams. Also playing was Bobby McAlinden who, though he never really made it as a player, would become George's best friend and team mate in America.

BUSBY BABES
On the other side of the city, Manchester United could smell the chance to reclaim the trophy they had previously considered to be theirs by right. The Busby Babes had won the FA Youth Cup for the first five years of its existence – from 1953 to 1957 – but since then the club had failed to even reach the final. This season the under-18s had progressed to the semi final by beating Barrow, Blackpool, Sheffield United and Wolves. Now, with silverware in sight, and two games against City all that separated them from the final, it was time to bring out the big gun – George Best was drafted back into the side.

It would be George's fourth game in a week, and this was perhaps why he did not shine as brilliantly in this game as he had begun to in the first team, but his mere presence in the ➤

👁 EYEWITNESS **What the players said...**
"The only real memory I have got of those two games was of Bestie. We got him in a corner, two of us, and he just turned and left us both for dead. He was incredible." **John Clay**

THE OPPOSITION

Mike Doyle

MANCHESTER CITY had just been relegated and it was Chelsea who had become the dominant force in youth football after the demise of the Busby Babes, but as the 1963-64 season developed it

became apparent that there were a number of very promising young players coming through at Maine Road. Five of this side had already made their first team debuts; Glyn Pardoe and David

David Connor

Connor would win Championship medals in 1968, and Mike Doyle would go on to play for England. City certainly had a team capable of winning the 1964 FA Youth Cup, if they could get past United...

Alan Ogley

David Sadler (left) and George Best, team mates tonight, would also play together in the 1968 European Cup final.

OFF THE PITCH **Number 1**

8 April 1964

The Beatles
Can't Buy Me Love

The Beatles
Can't Buy Me Love

fell for Albert Kinsey, the inside forward got ahead of his marker to guide the ball past Alan Ogley in the City goal.

This being a Manchester derby, however, it wasn't over yet. United continued to pepper the City goal but couldn't increase their lead. Then, just before half time and against the run of play, the prodigious Glyn Pardoe picked up the ball, went past three defenders, into the left-hand side of the penalty area, and hit a left-footed drive that struck the underside of the bar, crossed the line and then bounced back out of the goal. 1-1. Now it was the turn of the blue half of the stadium to erupt into a roar as deafening as it would have been for any first team encounter.

GULF IN CLASS

But blue joy was short-lived: the second half was even more one-sided and the gulf in class between the two sides began to show more and more with each United goal. Albert Kinsey's hat trick made him the hero of the night in the record books, but it was John Aston Junior who was the star, and George Best his inspiration.

With George Best in top form for the second leg, City were unable to reverse the deficit, losing 3-1 on the night and 7-2 on aggregate. Glyn Pardoe again equalised Mike Doyle's own goal before half time, but goals from Best and Sadler in the second half took United comfortably through to the final.

There, on 30 April, in front of another 25,000 fans, with George Best again outstanding, three David Sadler goals in the second leg at Old Trafford helped United to a 5-2 aggregate victory over Swindon Town. It was another hat-trick for another United player but Sadler doesn't take all the credit: "I remember in the final I scored three, and none of them was from outside the six-yard box, but Bestie won it. He was unstoppable."

The FA Youth Cup had gone to what half of Manchester considered to be its rightful home – and the young George Best had won his first piece of silverware. *Sporting* LEGENDS

➤ changing room was a massive boost for the other players. Though David Sadler had also already played for the first team, George Best was the team's talisman. "We had George," recalls John Aston. "And that meant we knew we were going to win."

Phil Burrows, whose job it was to mark Best that night, had played against him before. In Colin Shindler's excellent *George Best and 21 Others*, Burrows recalls an earlier B team match: "We kicked off, we lost possession, and this little skinny, dark-haired kid got hold of it, went round everyone and stuck it in the net. We kicked off again and the skinny kid got possession, went round everyone and scored. We lost 6-0, I think, but it was over in the first couple of minutes."

BRUISING ENCOUNTER

The match was a bruising encounter, played with all the passion of a first team game, and as soon as it began the pattern for both legs of the tie was quickly set. Willie Anderson and John Aston had the better of Mike Doyle and the right-footed David Wild, and when the first cross of the match

DID YOU KNOW?
Glyn Pardoe still holds the record for being Manchester City's youngest ever player. He was still 15 when he made his first-team debut in April 1962 and went on to make over 370 appearances for the club, until his career was prematurely ended by a leg-breaking George Best tackle in a derby match in December 1970.

THE RESULT

MANCHESTER UNITED	MANCHESTER CITY	
4	**1**	ATTENDANCE
Kinsey (3), Sadler	Pardoe	29,706

1964-1965

In his first full season as a first team player, George Best helps Manchester United win their first League Championship title since the success of the Busby Babes in 1957.

GEORGE BEST & THE FA CUP

"To my great regret, United never made it to a Cup final while I was there." **George Best**

For all that he achieved as a player, George Best was destined never to appear in an FA Cup final. The League and of course, the European Cup have always been better measures of how good a team actually is, but back then, rather more than nowadays, the FA Cup had, even for the biggest clubs, "a charisma that somehow the League never quite provided," as George himself once put it.

And playing in a Cup final was something the young George had always dreamed of. Back in the days before he signed professional terms at Old Trafford, while he was still moving around Manchester from one job to another, acting out the charade of being an amateur player in order to satisfy FA regulations, the idea that he might one day play in an FA Cup final was what got him through the day. "When I was at work, or

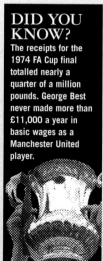

supposed to be working," he recalled, "I'd fantasize about games I was going to play in. It was always at Wembley; there were 100,000 people in the ground and it was a Cup final."

But even by then, though no one at Old Trafford ever doubted it, George was never sure enough of himself to believe that he might one day even make it as a pro, so the 1963 FA Cup final was a big day out for the lad.

TRIP TO WEMBLEY

The 1963 FA Cup final was played on 25 May, three days after George's 17th birthday, and so three days after he signed professional terms with the club. Manchester United were one game away from claiming their first major trophy since the Munich air disaster and, as he was now a member of the professional playing staff, George was taken to the match.

Before that day, his only experience of the FA Cup final had been watching it on television, which of course was all in black and white. The colour and spectacle of the occasion were to make a big impression on him: "Having had my appetite whetted by United's 1963 victory, it was a competition I longed to make it to the final of."

But it was never to be. The following season, with George now establishing himself in the team, Manchester United made it as far as the last hurdle, before being knocked out by West Ham; in 1965 they were beaten 1-0 by Leeds United in a semi final replay; and in 1966 it was Everton who

MANCHESTER UNITED'S FA CUP RECORD 1963-74
1963 Winners
1964 Semi finals
1965 Semi finals
1966 Semi finals
1967 Fourth round
1968 Third round
1969 Quarter finals
1970 Semi finals
1971 Third round
1972 Quarter finals
1973 Third round
1974 Fourth round

FA CUP FINALS 1963-74

1963	Manchester United **3** Leicester City **1**
1964	West Ham United **3** Preston North End **2**
1965	Liverpool **2** Leeds United **1** (aet)
1966	Everton **3** Sheffield Wednesday **2**
1967	Tottenham Hotspur **2** Chelsea **1**
1968	West Bromwich Albion **1** Everton **0** (aet)
1969	Manchester City **1** Leicester City **0**
1970	Chelsea **2** Leeds United **2**
1970 Replay	Chelsea **2** Leeds United **1** (aet)
1971	Arsenal **2** Liverpool **1** (aet)
1972	Leeds United **1** Arsenal **0**
1973	Sunderland **1** Leeds United **0**
1974	Liverpool **3** Newcastle United **0**

DID YOU KNOW?
The receipts for the 1974 FA Cup final totalled nearly a quarter of a million pounds. George Best never made more than £11,000 a year in basic wages as a Manchester United player.

went to Wembley after a 1-0 win at Burnden Park, then the home of Bolton Wanderers. Manchester United would never come as close again until 1970, when they were once again undone by Leeds United in the semi final – this time it took a second replay at Burnden Park before Billy Bremner scored the only goal of the encounter.

PLYMOUTH ARGYLE

And that would be as good as it got: it's a long story and we'll get to it later, but on 5 January 1974, Manchester United manager Tommy Docherty left George out of the team for the FA Cup third round match against Plymouth Argyle at Old Trafford.

The finest player of his generation walked out of the ground vowing never to play for Manchester United again. And he never did. *Sporting*LEGENDS

George Best (right) turns the ball into the net to score Manchester United's fourth and last goal against Barnsley in the fifth round of the 1964 FA Cup.

Date 30 SEPTEMBER 1964
Venue STAMFORD BRIDGE
Kick-off 8PM

CHELSEA

Sporting LEGENDS

George Best Match Programme
1964-1965

CHELSEA VS MANCHESTER UNITED

FOOTBALL CLUB

FOOTBALL LEAGUE DIVISION ONE

Bonetti

	Harris	Hinton	McCreadie
Shellito		Venables	Houseman
Murray	Hollins	Bridges	
	Tambling		

	Law	Herd	Connelly
Best	Charlton	Crerand	Brennan
A Dunne	Stiles	Foulkes	
	P Dunne		

FOOTBALL LEAGUE DIVISION ONE

Chelsea
VS
Manchester United

VENUE	Stamford Bridge
DATE	Wednesday, 30 September 1964
KICK-OFF	8.00pm

This was the game when George Best first realised that something exceptional was happening to him. He scored the first goal and made the second. He was becoming the new star player in a team of stars. Football had always been easy, but when he found that it was still easy away to one of the best teams in the country, he began to realise that he was playing for a team that would become special, and that he would become special with it.

Opposing full back Ken Shellito was a cultured player and England international in his prime but George turned him and his partner Eddie McCreadie, a Scotland international, this way and that, standing still when it looked like he was about to show his pace and then darting off when it looked like he was going to stand still.

Chelsea started the game briskly, with Terry Venables orchestrating their attacks from the centre of the pitch. But United closed the playmaker down, forcing him ever deeper into his own half. The away team slowly began to get a grip on the game and after half an hour Chelsea were hit on the break. With their centre halves still forward for a corner, Pat Crerand found Denis

DID YOU KNOW?

George Best would play in all but one of Manchester United's League games in 1964/65 and score a highly respectable ten goals. He would also play seven FA Cup games and eleven Fairs Cup games, adding four more goals to his tally. Shay Brennan, John Connelly, Tony Dunne and Bill Foulkes were all ever-present in the first eleven throughout the season.

Law, who headed the ball on. McCreadie tried to pass the ball back to Bonetti but George Best anticipated the move and his blistering acceleration allowed him to cut out the pass and slot the ball home.

CHIPPED CROSS

The second half started as the first did, with Chelsea attacking and United just trying to cope. But again, the Reds slowly got into the game and could have gone 2-0 up when Charlton hit the bar with a bullet header; then David Herd should have scored from the edge of the six-yard box. In the end, it was up to the brilliance of Best to seal the victory. Picking up the ball 30 yards out, he went past his marker and fed Denis Law with a delightful chipped cross into the area. Bonetti got his fingertips to it but it wasn't enough. ➤

👁 EYEWITNESS What the manager said...

"It was one of the many great displays he gave at Chelsea. Something about the ground used to lift him, make him play better. But I shall always remember that first time." **Matt Busby**

THE OPPOSITION

John Hollins

THERE WAS a lot of interest in this game at the time. The season was barely a month old but it was already beginning to look like the eventual champions would come either from one of these clubs

or Leeds. There was also a marked contrast of styles for the aficionado to savour: Chelsea played the hard-running style that was fast becoming fashionable in England at the time; Matt Busby's

Terry Venables

Manchester United still played with the attacking flair of yesteryear, where individual brilliance rather than hard work as a unit was expected to win matches and entertain fans. Tonight it did both.

Ken Shellito

➤ Law was one of the finest goalscorers of his generation and the Scotsman leapt up to head the ball home and win the match.

Chelsea looked like title contenders but everything Best tried against them that night came off. At the end of the game, Ken Shellito ran over to congratulate him on his performance. Other opposition players came to pat him on the back and both sets of fans applauded him off the pitch.

INTERNATIONAL DUTY

The following morning, George woke up alone in the President Hotel in Russell Square to find his name all over the papers. His room mate David Sadler and the rest of the team were already on their way back to Manchester. George had stayed in London to catch a flight to Belfast later that day. Still only 18, he had been selected to play for Northern Ireland against England on Saturday. It would be his third cap. He took his time, drinking tea and reading the morning papers, in

Chelsea goalkeeper Peter Bonetti jumps and reaches for the ball as it rebounds down from the crossbar after a Dennis Law header.

which he featured heavily. The report in *The Times* was as flowery as any: "Shellito, in particular, must have felt that he was trying to push a genie back into its bottle." (Pat Crerand's appraisal was rather more grisly and vivid: "Shellito was taken off suffering from twisted blood.")

The *Daily Mirror* had the final say: "Head down on his chest, the little Irishman shambled into the tunnel. It was over."

SHYNESS

That, he has said, was the precise moment when it hit him; when he realised just how far his career could go. He was playing in a team capable of taking Chelsea apart at Stamford Bridge; he was becoming established in the Northern Ireland side, and, as the newspapers kept reminding him, he had just played a match where everything he tried seemed to come off. He was also about to discover that he was losing some of his shyness with the girls.

Going over to the window to watch the world go by, he sees two blonde girls on the Square

⏱ OFF THE PITCH
On this day

The Soviet Union commissions the first unit of the Novovoronezh Nuclear Power Plant. Five nuclear power units will eventually be built at the site.

below. It seems strange, but he's sure they're looking at him. The girls back in Belfast never paid him any attention. So, quite out of character, and just because he just feels so good that morning, he waves at them. And sure enough, one of them waves back. That makes him smile, which makes the girl and her friend laugh. He's pulled. And he hasn't even finished his breakfast yet. Looking quickly around the room he finds a paper blotter on the desk, on which he writes his room number in big numbers. This he holds up against the window. The phone rang before he'd even replaced the blotter on the desk. She was Swedish, as it turned out.

England won 4-3 on the Saturday, as everyone thought they would. But having taken a 4-0 lead by the interval thanks to a hat trick from Jimmy Greaves, the second half was all about Northern Ireland and George Best, a young man who was about to win his first League Championship winner's medal. *Sporting*LEGENDS

THE RESULT		
	CHELSEA	MANCHESTER UNITED
ATTENDANCE 60,769	**0**	**2** Best, Law

FOOTBALL LEAGUE DIVISION ONE

Manchester United
VS
Chelsea

VENUE	Old Trafford
DATE	Saturday, 13 March 1965
KICK-OFF	3pm

According to George Best in the last book he wrote before he died, *Hard Tackles and Dirty Baths*, what actually cost Chelsea the League in 1965 was not just the form of Manchester United and Leeds United but a certain drinking accident involving eight of their first team squad. Disobeying orders from Tommy Docherty the players had sneaked out of the team hotel one night and soon found themselves ensconced in a late-night bar. Despite the enormity of their behaviour, it all would have gone without a hitch, except that Docherty caught them as they were coming back into the hotel.

In those days, it was far more common for clubs to impose their own sanctions on any players who stepped out of line – as George would find

Having just beaten George's boyhood heroes Wolves twice in the space of a fortnight – 3-0 at home in the League and 5-3 at Molineux in the FA Cup – Manchester United were defending a home League record that had seen them unbeaten since a 1-0 reverse by Leeds United on 5 December. They would remain unbeaten at home for the remainder of the League season.

out later on in his career – and, fearing for the good name of the club, Tommy Docherty immediately suspended all eight revellers. Needless to say, results deteriorated. Five of the players were later recalled to the side, but this Chelsea team was a team that depended heavily on organisation and team spirit, and the team had been broken up.

Chelsea would have the consolation of winning the League Cup this season, but another defeat by Manchester United in the League, and this time by an even more convincing score line, would go a long way to ending their hopes of winning a second League title, ten years after their first.

GOOD FORM

Manchester United came into the game on good form. They had just registered two wins against Wolverhampton Wanderers, one in the League and one in the FA Cup, and had scored eight goals in the process. But Wolves, with all respect, ➤

> *"I would usually be up against the full back, though other sides would designate a man marker. Arsenal would usually put Peter Storey on me, while Chelsea had their hatchet man Chopper Harris."* **George Best**

THE OPPOSITION

Peter Bonetti

RECOVERING FROM the defeat by Manchester United in September, Chelsea had led the way in the League throughout the season and by now would have been starting to really fancy their chances.

Eddie McCreadie

Tommy Docherty's side were as talented as they were hard-working, and with the likes of George Graham, John Hollins and Terry Venables in the team, they were well organised too. Most neutrals,

however, wanted Manchester United to win the title – not just because of the groundswell of sympathy that had arisen out of Munich but also because Matt Busby insisted on playing attractive football.

Barry Bridges

Peter Bonetti and Chopper Harris work together to keep the ball out of the net in a corresponding fixture in March 1968. George Best (second right) looks on.

➤ were very much a team in decline – they would be relegated with Birmingham City at the end of the season, just six years after winning back-to-back League titles. Chelsea, on the other hand, despite their two hedefeats to Manchester United this season, were always a different proposition.

HARD MAN

Every team had a hard man – even silky Manchester United had Billy Foulkes and Nobby Stiles – but Chopper Harris was a class apart. He never pretended to be a ball-playing footballer. In another match between Manchester United and Chelsea, in 1970, George scored a goal against him that typifies, perhaps more than any other, everything that George Best was about.

There is not a single professional player playing today who could score a goal like this one, because there is not a single player playing today who would still have been on his feet to put the ball into the net. Their managers wouldn't allow it for a start. You've been fouled in a goal scoring position: you go down. Then you either writhe around for five minutes or you leap up holding an imaginary card while your friends hit your opponents with their imaginary handbags. But George didn't take free kicks, so his only chance of scoring was to stay on his feet.

It began when George chased after an ineffective clearance. Then his gamble paid off when he was put through on goal after a poor backpass. With only the goalie to beat, Best prepares to shoot. Then Chopper Harris arrives.

The better a player was the more he got

kicked. Pelé, for example, got kicked right out of the 1962 World Cup. George Best also took his fair share of stud marks, but the trick was to never let your opponent know you'd been hurt; to always go back for more and, if the opportunity arose, perhaps to knock the ball between his legs a couple of times. That's what really got to people like Chopper Harris.

Chopper sees the danger, and perhaps some red mist, and rushes back from the left-half position. He then tries to go straight through George's legs. There would be allegations later that he genuinely tried to injure his opponent in the tackle, but what is sure is that he had absolutely no intention of playing the ball.

But Best sees him coming and, with no more than a shimmy of the hips, he evades the brunt of the assault, wobbles slightly as he regains his balance, and then resumes his conversation with the football. It's not enough for him then to simply slot the ball past Peter Bonetti, however. He has to take it to the tips of the keeper's fingers, before tapping it past him and, from a tight angle, rolling it gently into the net just before the defence can recover. *Sporting*LEGENDS

THE RESULT

MANCHESTER UNITED	CHELSEA
4	**0**
Herd (2), Best, Law	ATTENDANCE 56,261

LEAGUE CHAMPIONS *1965*

There was a quiet mood of cold determination in the Manchester United dressing room at the start of the 1964/65 campaign. George didn't have the experience yet to fully understand but the older heads were already aware that this team was capable of achieving great things. They had a forward line that was the envy of the First Division and as long as they could keep it tight at the back they knew they were in with a chance of winning the League.

There were rivals for the Championship, though, and plenty of them. As well as Chelsea, no one could discount FA Cup holders West Ham,

Manchester United centre forward David Herd (centre) throws up his arms as his shot shakes the top of the Chelsea net for Manchester United's second goal in the match at Old Trafford. Peter Bonetti, on his knees, can only watch the ball fly into the net.

or reigning champions Liverpool. And then there was Leeds. Having signed Manchester United's winger Johnny Giles in the summer of 1963, and putting him into the centre of midfield, where he was forging an effective partnership with Billy Bremner, the Yorkshire team had won promotion the following season and would go on this year to take the First Division by storm.

THE BATTLE OF GOODISON PARK
George never liked Leeds United, and was always quite open about it. He tells us it's because they were a dirty team – and, in fairness, when they went to Everton that season, things got so ➤

"From the very beginning of the 1964/65 season he played with a confidence that was startling in one so young and revealed a staggering variety of skills sufficient to make the most discriminating connoisseur drool at the very mention of his name." **Michael Parkinson**

➤ heated that the referee had to order both teams off the pitch before half time and hold the game up for a full ten minutes to allow the players to calm down. Furthermore, like Chelsea, Leeds had adopted the style of play that had taken Alf Ramsey's Ipswich Town side to the Championship in 1962; they were efficient, above all else, much like the England team that would win the World Cup in 1966. But perhaps the real reason for his dislike of Leeds was that Leeds had Paul Reaney, the only full back in the game who could cope with George's trickery.

CONSISTENCY

Leeds would have to wait, however: this was to be Manchester United's season, though in the end it came down to goal average. After a shaky start in which they took only two points from their three August games, Matt Busby's side started getting results. The key was the consistency of the line up. Pat Dunne played in goal; the full backs were

DID YOU KNOW?
The 1964/65 campaign was Sir Stanley Matthews final season as a player. Having made his debut as a 17-year-old as long ago as March 1932, the great man, who was still playing in the First Division for Stoke City, retired at the quite remarkable age of 50.

Shay Brennan and Tony Dunne; the central defensive partnership was made up of Bill Foulkes and Nobby Stiles; Pat Crerand held the midfield; while John Connelly, David Herd, Bobby Charlton, Denis Law and George Best took turns in terrorising defences. Denis Law ended the season as top scorer with 28 League goals; Herd got 20; Connelly 15; while Best and Charlton both weighed in with a healthy tally of 10 each.

It went to the wire, as everyone thought it would, but free-scoring Manchester United were the most exciting team in the League and deserving champions. *Sporting*LEGENDS

LEAGUE DIVISION ONE 1964/1965 FINAL TABLE							
	P	W	D	L	F	A	PTS
Manchester United	42	26	9	7	89	39	61
Leeds United	42	26	9	7	83	52	61
Chelsea	42	24	8	10	89	54	56

George Best takes on Liverpool goalkeeper Tommy Lawrence as Denis Law (right) looks on. Manchester United vs Liverpool. 24 April 1965.

© Colorsport

1965-1966

Though he would miss the World Cup in England, 1965/66 was the year in which George Best was transformed from highly promising outside forward into the most famous name in British football.

GEORGE BEST & THE WORLD CUP

"Bestie only needed five or ten minutes in his first training session to make his mark. We were all looking at each other, raising our eyebrows, within those first five minutes." **Terry Neil**

Perhaps the most telling statistic about George Best's international career is that Pat Jennings, who made his Northern Ireland debut on the same day as George, went on to win a record 119 caps, while George played only 37 times for his country. On the day that George became the youngest ever player to wear the green, Jennings also came into the side for Manchester United legend Harry Gregg, who was

Above: the Northern Ireland team that made it as far as the quarter finals of the 1958 World Cup in Sweden.

dropped after an 8-3 defeat by England in the previous game.

To be fair, Pat was a goalkeeper, and it is unlikely that George, for whom pace and acceleration were important parts of his game, could ever have played on that long, however well he'd looked after himself. But if he'd been able to play on until his mid-30s, he would have realised his ambition to play in a World Cup finals. In fact, if he'd made the trip to Moscow in 1969, he

George Best scores past Switzerland's goalkeeper Elsener in the 1964 World Cup Qualifier.

GEORGE BEST'S INTERNATIONAL CAREER 37 caps, 9 goals					
Date	Tournament	Opponents	Venue	Result	Goals
15 April 1964	Home International	Wales	(A)	3-2	
29 April 1964	Friendly	Uruguay	(H)	3-0	
3 October 1964	Home International	England	(H)	3-4	
14 October 1964	World Cup qualifier	Switzerland	(H)	1-0	
14 November 1964	World Cup qualifier	Switzerland	(A)	1-2	1
25 November 1964	Home International	Scotland	(A)	2-3	1
17 March 1965	World Cup qualifier	Netherlands	(H)	2-1	
7 April 1965	World Cup qualifier	Netherlands	(A)	0-0	
7 May 1965	World Cup qualifier	Albania	(H)	4-1	1
2 October 1965	Home International	Scotland	(H)	3-2	
10 November 1965	Home International	England	(A)	1-2	
24 November 1965	World Cup qualifier	Albania	(A)	1-1	
22 October 1966	European Champ qualifier	England	(H)	0-2	
21 October 1967	European Champ qualifier	Scotland	(H)	1-0	
23 October 1968	World Cup qualifier	Turkey	(H)	4-1	1
3 May 1969	Home International	England	(H)	1-3	
6 May 1969	Home International	Scotland	(A)	1-1	
10 May 1969	Home International	Wales	(H)	0-0	
10 September 1969	World Cup qualifier	USSR	(H)	0-0	
18 April 1970	Home International	Scotland	(H)	0-1	
21 April 1970	Home International	England	(A)	1-3	1
25 April 1970	Home International	Wales	(A)	0-1	
11 November 1970	European Champ qualifier	Spain	(A)	0-3	
3 February 1971	European Champ qualifier	Cyprus	(A)	3-0	1
21 April 1971	European Champ qualifier	Cyprus	(H)	5-0	3
15 May 1971	Home International	England	(H)	0-1	
18 May 1971	Home International	Scotland	(A)	1-0	
22 May 1971	Home International	Wales	(H)	1-0	
22 September 1971	European Champ qualifier	USSR	(A)	0-1	
16 February 1972	European Champ qualifier	Spain	(H)	1-1	
18 October 1972	World Cup qualifier	Bulgaria	(A)	0-3	
14 November 1973	World Cup qualifier	Portugal	(A)	1-1	
13 October 1976	World Cup qualifier	Netherlands	(A)	2-2	
10 November 1976	World Cup qualifier	Belgium	(A)	0-2	
27 April 1977	Friendly	West Germany	(A)	0-5	
21 September 1977	World Cup qualifier	Iceland	(H)	2-0	
12 October 1977	World Cup qualifier	Netherlands	(H)	0-1	

might well have played in a World Cup while he was still in his prime.

CLUB VERSUS COUNTRY

Forty years is a long time in football, but one thing that hasn't changed is the nature of what is known as 'the old club-versus-country debate'. It happened several times, the most notorious being the last game of the qualifying campaign for the 1970 World Cup. Having beaten Turkey twice and earned a draw against the Soviets in Belfast, Northern Ireland needed a draw on a Wednesday night in Moscow to qualify for the finals.

But George 'picked up a knock' playing for Manchester United against Burnley in a League Cup match on the Monday and was withdrawn from the squad. The Irish lost 2-0. George came in for quite a lot of stick when he turned out to play against West Bromwich Albion the following Saturday. The feeling was that if George had been playing for England, not only would the English FA have been able to put enough pressure on Matt Busby to have him released by the club, but that there was no way he would have been expected to play for his club two days before an international match of such importance.

But perhaps it wasn't all about Matt Busby. George was often obviously not happy at having to play with inferior players: "We always had four or five decent players from the top clubs, but had to make up the numbers with lads from the Second or Third Division – sometimes even the Irish League," he complained. *Sporting*LEGENDS

*Sporting*LEGENDS

George Best Match Programme 1965-1966

BENFICA

MANCHESTER UNITED

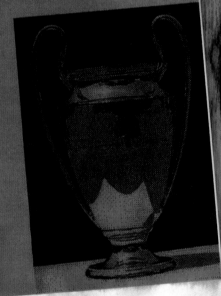

Date **9 March 1966**
Venue **Estadio da Luz**
Kick-off **9pm**

EUROPEAN CUP QUARTER FINAL SECOND LEG

Costa Pereira

Cavem   Germano   Pinto   Cruz

José Augusto   Coluna   Augusto Silva   Simoes

Eusebio   Torres

Law   Herd

Charlton   Crerand   Best

Connelly   Foulkes   Brennan

Dunne   Stiles

Gregg

∾ EUROPEAN CUP QUARTER FINAL SECOND LEG ∾

Benfica
VS
Manchester United

VENUE	Estadio da Luz
DATE	Wednesday, 9 March 1966
KICK-OFF	9pm

Y ou'll no doubt be aware that the only way to deal with Continental opposition, especially away from home, is to keep it tight for the first twenty. You can't just go flying off down the wing, taking people on and playing open, free-flowing football, because when they do get the ball off you, as they inevitably will, you won't see it again for the next quarter of an hour. And that's exactly Matt Busby told his players just before they stepped out into the cauldron of flares and smoke and 100,000 baying foreigners that was the Stadium of Light.

Even the understated Bobby Charlton admits to having felt "a little bit of trepidation, about what we should expect, going to the Stadium of Light". And when the away team coach had arrived at the stadium, it was met by fans who held five fingers up to the window, to remind the Manchester United team of the crushing defeat their city rivals Sporting Lisbon had inflicted on the English club two years before.

This time the advantage they took to Portugal was nothing to compare: Manchester United held only a meagre 3-2 lead from the first leg at Old

DID YOU KNOW?
In the away changing room just before the game was due to kick off, Manchester United's Paddy Crerand was bouncing a ball repeatedly against the wall to try to calm his nerves when the giant mirror that was hanging there fell to the ground and shattered all over the floor.

Trafford and any kind of result would be a major achievement. Nerves were jangling. Except for George's (George's nerves never jangled). And anyway, the man whose night it would become obviously wasn't even listening to his manager before the game, because within ten minutes he had single-handedly won the tie with two wonderful individual goals.

LENGTH OF THE PITCH
The first came out of nowhere and before the game had settled into a pattern. About thirty yards out from his own goal, George breaks up an early Benfica attack with a timely header and then charges off on his own down the middle of ➤

👁 EYEWITNESS What the players said...

"He was at his peak. He was so fast and so brave, he would go into tackles and win balls that you never really expected him to get. And that particular match was the best I ever saw him play." **Bobby Charlton**

THE OPPOSITION

THE NAME of Benfica was already legendary. The Portuguese side had won the European Cup in 1961 and 1962 and had reached the final in 1963 and 1965 – and they had never lost a European match at home.

Germano

Their influential skipper Coluna scored freely from midfield, their aptly named centre forward Torres stood two metres tall, and Eusebio had just been named European player of the year. Benfica were mysterious

Eusebio

giants; they were held in awe but virtually unknown in Britain, where European club matches not involving British teams were rarely shown on television. This game, however, would be shown over and over again.

Pinto

quick-minded enough to be advancing through the centre circle can run onto it.

PACE

Best is there. He controls it as it bounces with his right, then suddenly it's on his left. He completely outstrips two white shirts for pace and side-steps the out-stretched leg of a third. "He just kept going and running past everybody," says Paddy Crerand. "I just stood there and watched because there was no way George was going to pass the ball to anyone."

George charges on into the area and, without breaking stride, calmly clips the ball past Costa Pereira and into the back of the net. As the television camera tries to keep up, it overshoots the action, so now the archive footage shows a row of people just behind the goal. And they're all very, very quiet.

George is too. There are no histrionics: no running to the corner flag with his shirt off and his muscles taut. He just hangs his head and starts the long walk back to his own half of the pitch. Denis Law and David Herd come over and pat him on the head. The rest of his team mates just stand there and gape in admiration. High above the action in the press box is the *Manchester Evening News* reporter David Meek: "It was so audacious and unexpected. I remember leaping to my feet, against all the etiquette of the press box."

GAME OVER

The game was over, almost before it had begun. Already 2-0 up, Manchester United gain in confidence and within half an hour they've gone three up after a string of passes and a brave David Herd header puts John Connelly through. Denis Law follows the ball into the net and then bangs both his fists on the turf in triumph.

Benfica offer their own fans a faint glimmer of hope when they pull one back after half time through an own goal by Shay Brennan, but it's never going to be enough. Crerand gets in behind the defence to make it four and then Bobby Charlton goes round the keeper and ends the scoring with a goal George himself would have been proud of.

At the final whistle, the Portuguese fans invade the pitch and charge towards George. One of them has a knife – but he doesn't doesn't mean any harm to the hero of the night: he just wants a lock of that Beatle hair. *Sporting*LEGENDS

➤ the pitch. A second header controls the ball as he crosses the halfway line, now in full flight. It takes a foul on Bobby Charlton to halt United's progress halfway inside the Benfica half. Tony Dunne takes the free kick left-footed and floats it in towards the penalty spot – and it's George Best who gets ahead of his marker and whose looping header sails over the out-coming Costa Pereira and into the back of the net.

Six minutes later, Harry Gregg punts the ball out down the middle and finds David Herd in acres of space. Herd does what any target man should do in such a situation: he heads the ball down in the hope that anyone who might be

George Best wearing a souvenir sombrero on his return to London following Manchester United's defeat of Benfica in the second leg of the European Cup quarter final.

⏱ OFF THE PITCH On this day

North Vietnamese troops attack US Green Berets at A Shau, a camp set up near the Laotian border to stem the flow of enemy troops into Vietnam along the Ho Chi Minh Trail. There are heavy casualties on both sides during the two days of fighting that follow before the fall of the camp.

THE RESULT

	BENFICA	MANCHESTER UNITEED
ATTENDANCE 100,000	**1** Brennan (og),	**5** Best (2), Connelly, Crerand, Charlton

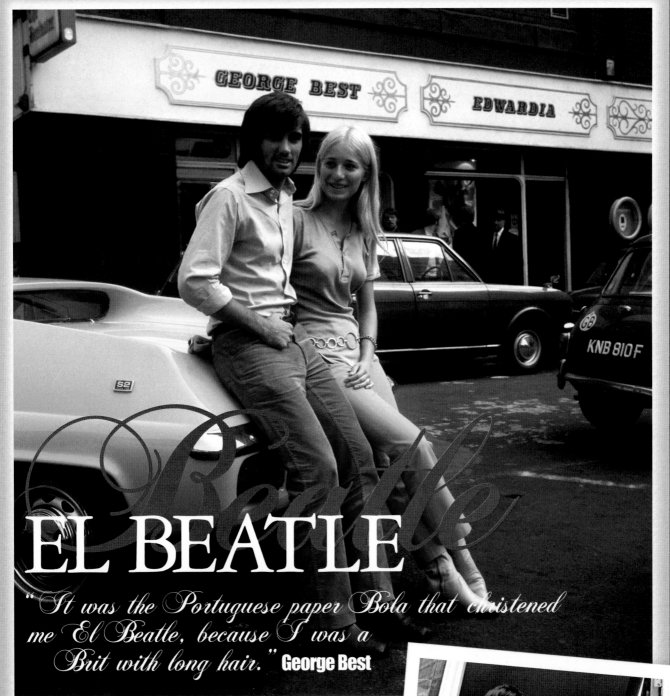

EL BEATLE

"It was the Portuguese paper Bola that christened me El Beatle, because I was a Brit with long hair." **George Best**

The story of George Best's courtship of Eva Haraldsted is quite revealing. The couple were, for a while, engaged to be married. It appears that Eva thought that this was quite a good idea, though for George's part, it all seems to have been something of an accident.

Long before Georgie Best Superstar had become a household name throughout Britain and Ireland there were inklings that the youngster had a wayward bent; that he didn't always behave in a way befitting a first-class athlete. That in itself wasn't unusual in a footballing culture where drinking was seen as a team-bonding enterprise and quite often actively encouraged by managers.

But George was always capable of going one step further – when everybody else had had enough and was ready to go home, he was ➤

Above: George with Eva Haraldsted outside his boutique on Manchester's Bridge Street.

Right: George with Manchester City star Mike Summerbee inside their boutique.

George and Mike Summerbee

Above: George giving the final set to one of his creations before a fashion show at Tiffany's.

Left: George enjoys a drink with his parents.

Mum, dad and George raise a toast

> always the one looking for another bar to go to. This proclivity hadn't gone unnoticed at Old Trafford. Indeed, Denis Law had been called up before Matt Busby when he had gone off the rails, and had taken heed of the warning.

Busby suggested to George that he should settle down. George didn't want to go against the wishes of his manager, so he went out and proposed to the first woman he met.

BREACH OF CONTRACT

"That wasn't quite what I meant," said Busby, who had heard about the engagement through the newspapers. George was confused – not because he had misinterpreted his manager, but because Eva was a very beautiful woman, as you can see. But, no, when he thought about it, he didn't actually want to marry her. He was too young for ➤

"When I think back, they were probably the happiest days of my life, in 1966 and '67. Talk about fulfilling a dream!" **George Best**

Above: George with the actress Susan George on holiday in Spain.

Left: George is besieged by young autograph hunters during training for an international against England.

George signs for fans

that. So he called it off. And Eva sued him for breach of contract. And won.

"TELL ME, GEORGE…"
You'll surely understand that the combination of fame, money, youth, good looks and your own shirt in the dressing room of arguably the most famous football club in the world could give a man the impression that life was just a beatiful dream. Which is why, perhaps, that when, many years later, a Belfast-born bellboy came into his hotel room to find George in bed with Miss World and gambling winnings totalling more than several thousand pounds in cash strewn about the place, and famously asked him: "Tell me George, where did it all go wrong?" it took him over a decade to work out that it was meant as a serious question. *Sporting*LEGENDS

"I would say that the media were maybe a bit to blame. They drove him mental. They wouldn't leave him alone wherever he went or whatever he'd done." **Pat Crerand**

1966-1967

Though success in Europe continues to elude them, with the universally feared strike force of Bobby Charlton, Denis Law and George Best leading the line, Manchester United win their second League Championship in three seasons.

Sporting **LEGENDS**

GEORGE BEST MATCH PROGRAMME

1966-1967

Date **10 December 1966**
Venue **Old Trafford**
Kick-off **3pm**

MANCHESTER **UNITED** vs **LIVERPOOL**

FOOTBALL LEAGUE DIVISION ONE

Stepney

Brennan   A Dunne   Sadler   Noble

Ryan   Crerand   Charlton   Aston

Best   Herd

St John

Hunt   Milne   Callaghan

Thompson   Stevenson   Smith   Lawler

Strong   Yeats

Lawrence

❧ LEAGUE DIVISION ONE ❧
Manchester United
VS
Liverpool

VENUE	Old Trafford
DATE	Saturday, 10 December 1966
KICK-OFF	3pm

DID YOU KNOW?
On the Wednesday before this match, Liverpool had travelled to a foggy Amsterdam to play Ajax in the European Cup. The Dutch had won 5-1, scoring four of their goals in the first half.

"At twenty enthusiasm reigns, at thirty the wit and at forty the judgement," Sir Matt Busby once said. Sadly, it wouldn't work out that way for George Best but at least his club manager had got the first bit right. He wouldn't turn 21 until the end of the season, yet George Best had already made more than 100 appearances for Manchester United in the League and was fast approaching the 150-mark in all competitions. He had already been a first team regular for three years and that match in Estoril towards the end of the previous season had made him an even more high profile player than his illustrious team mates Bobby Charlton and Denis Law. Indeed, he was the hottest property the game of football had ever known. There had been footballing superstars before – Tom Finney, Stanley Matthews, and Denis Law had all been household names – but nobody had ever crossed the line between football and popular culture in the way that George did.

WE WANT GEORGIE!
One month after the match against Sporting Lisbon, George opened a boutique in Sale. He had always been interested in clothes and this was part of his appeal as something more than a football player: "I was the one wearing the Chelsea boots, the square waistcoats, the turn-back cuffs and the tailored shirts," he admitted. "At least when I began in the boutique business I had no great illusions of making money. It was only a little shop and both Malcolm Mooney, my partner, and I knew it would never be our fortune." Never the less, his initial foray into the rag trade looked like it would get off to a good start: two hours before the suburban shop opened there was a large crowd of fans, mostly schoolgirls, waiting outside the shop to get a glimpse of the superstar.

It got worse: in November, George went with Bobby Charlton and Nobby Stiles to the opening of the New Market Centre in Manchester. "It was like a riot," recalled George. "Something like a thousand people were there, quite a lot of them women with young children taking a break ➤

👁 EYEWITNESS **What the managers said...**
"George, son, some advice: don't be too demanding, because it's a sad fact of life that genius is born and not paid." **Bill Shankly**

THE OPPOSITION

Ian St John

WHEN BILL SHANKLY took over as manager in 1959 Liverpool were floundering in the Second Dvision. By 1966/67 they had become one of the main forces in English football – the Merseysiders

had won the League in 1964 and 1966 and the FA Cup in 1965. They would eventually slip to 5th place in the final League table this season, but in the run-up to Christmas 1966 the title holders were

Roger Hunt

still vying with Manchester United for top spot. It was still too early to tell for sure, but this meeting between two great sides at Old Trafford had all the makings of a Championship decider.

Ian Callaghan

Liverpool's Roger Hunt is challenged by Tony Dunne in the corresponding fixture at Anfield in March 1967. The match ended in a 0-0 draw.

© Colorsport

➤ from their shopping. The police tried to control it, but all of a sudden there were scarf-waving fans rushing everywhere and girls shouting 'We want Georgie!'" It all became too much for Nobby, who had to go and hide in the post office to get away from George's fans.

EVER PRESENT

But despite his obvious appeal to people who had little or no interest in football, most of the action still took place on the pitch. Both George Best and Bobby Charlton played in all 42 of Manchester United's League matches this season, but a further two appearances in the FA Cup and one in the League Cup made George the team's

DID YOU KNOW?
In September 1966 Manchester United signed Alex Stepney from Chelsea as a replacement for Harry Gregg, who moved to Stoke City as player-coach in December.

OFF THE PITCH Number 1

10 December 1966

The Beatles
Hello Goodbye

The Monkees
Daydream Believer

busiest player with 45 appearances in total. He was also starting to become a reliable goal scorer. George's two goals today, matched by a brace from the Liverpool centre forward Ian St John, earned both teams a point. They also brought his tally for the season so far to six, and his career total to 42 in all competitions. *Sporting*LEGENDS

OFF THE PITCH On this day

The United Nations General Assembly adopts international covenants that are designed to give legal weight to the Universal Declaration of Human Rights.

THE RESULT

MANCHESTER UNITED	LIVERPOOL
2	**2**
Best (2)	St John (2)

ATTENDANCE
61,768

ANTHEM PUBLISHING AND TOFFS – The Old Fashioned Football Company – have teamed up to offer readers of George Best – His Greatest Games, 10% off any order.

TOFFS manufactures and sells some of the finest reproduction football shirts available and has a range of high quality George Best related products. From the 1963 FA Cup Final shirt where George was but a spectator, to the 1968 European Cup Final, United and Northern Ireland shirts of the 70s, and even the LA Aztecs, TOFFS has something distinctive for every fan of George's.

SPECIAL OFFER 10% OFF

Find out more online at www.toffs.com, call

08450 6 1966 6

or +44 (0)191 4913500 outside the UK.

WEST HAM UNITED

MANCHESTER UNITED

Date **6 May 1967**

Venue **Upton Park**   Kick-off **3pm**

FOOTBALL LEAGUE DIVISION ONE

Mackleworth

Charles   Moore   Heffer   Burkett

Sissons   Peters   Boyce   Redknapp

Hurst   Bennett

Best

Law   Charlton   Crerand

Aston   Sadler   Foulkes   Brennan

A Dunne   Stiles

Stepney

GEORGE BEST MATCH PROGRAMME 1966-1967

FOOTBALL LEAGUE DIVISION ONE

West Ham United
VS
Manchester United

VENUE	Upton Park
DATE	Saturday, 6 May 1967
KICK-OFF	3pm

West Ham United's season was effectively over. They were far too good to go down but defensively they were not solid – they conceded an average of two goals a game in 1966/67 and would finish the season in 16th place. Manchester United, on the other hand, could claim a second League title in three years with just a draw today. As it turned out they would do rather better than that and would win the League in some style, and with a home game against Stoke City to spare.

Tottenham Hotspur and Chelsea would battle it out at Wembley for the FA Cup but, as Bob Ferrier of *The Observer* would state in his report of this match: "If the capital is to have the Cup final, then Manchester is once again the centre of the universe." And the three indestructible stars at the

Unbeaten in the League since a 2-1 defeat against Sheffield United at Bramall Lane on Boxing Day, the newly-crowned champions would finish the 1966/67 season with a 0-0 home draw against Stoke City. Their only defeat to date in 1967 had been a 2-1 reverse at home to Norwich City in the fourth round of the FA Cup.

centre of that universe were the red-shirted forward line of Charlton, Law and Best – all of whom would shine today.

BOBBY CHARLTON THUNDERBOLT

Bobby Charlton opened the scoring after just two minutes. Law played the ball through to Nobby Stiles; Stiles was tackled but the ball squirmed out and broke for Charlton. It was only a half chance at best but Charlton got between two defenders and hit one of his trademark thunderbolts. Young Colin Mackleworth, who was playing only his second League game, stood no chance.

The Reds went two up five minutes later when John Aston Junior crossed for Paddy Crerand, who headed the ball firmly beyond Mackleworth's outstretched hand. Then, just three minutes later, Manchester United won a corner. Bill Foulkes challenged the goalkeeper and when the ball came down it fell for the Manchester United centre half, who turned and lashed the ball home to make it 3-0. Only ten minutes of the game had been played, but the result – and the destination ➤

"My goal against West Ham was my tenth of the season, which may not seem a lot after I'd played in all 42 League games, but I probably made twice as many for Denis and the other players." **George Best**

THE OPPOSITION

WEST HAM UNITED were the darlings of the British media in the 1966/67 season – and indeed, the English public at large. Three of their players – Moore,

Hurst and Peters – had been an integral part of the England team that had just won the World Cup, and the Hammers were an exciting team too. They never achieved

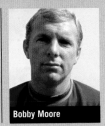
Bobby Moore

the consistency in the League to make a serious title challenge but they had been FA Cup winners in 1964, had gone on to win the European Cup Winners Cup in

1965 and had reached the semi finals of that competition in 1966. "We believed in attacking, win or lose," said Sir Geoff Hurst later. Today they would lose.

Geoff Hurst

Paddy Crerand jumps with Bobby Charlton to head Manchester United's second goal, watched by George Best (second left). The West Ham defenders are Peter Bennett (8) and John Bond (4).

OFF THE PITCH Number 1
6 May 1967

Sandie Shaw
Puppet On A String

Nancy and Frank Sinatra
Something Stupid

survivor of the Munich air disaster who had made his debut in 1952 and had already won two League Championship medals with Manchester United in 1956 and 1957. After the sixth goal went in Nobby Stiles trotted over to the big man and said: "Congratulations, Bill, on your fourth Championship medal." But the former mineworker just turned round and gave the World Cup winner "a right rollicking" and told him to "concentrate on the game". Like West Ham were going to come back from that. *Sporting*LEGENDS

EYEWITNESS What the papers said...

"This may not be United's greatest Championship win, their greatest team. But certainly in the history of the club they can never have had such devestating forwards as Charlton, Law and Best." The Observer

➤ of the League Championship trophy — was no longer in question.

A quarter of an hour later there was more. And this time it came from the boot of George Best. Nobby Stiles cut inside Jack Burkett and, sensibly, gave the ball to Best. George controlled it with his right foot, then suddenly it was on his left, and then it was in the back of the net, under the despairing young keeper who now lay forlornly in the mud.

JOHNNY THE ONE

To their credit, West Ham came out after the break still prepared to play football, and their endeavours were rewarded almost immediately with a John Charles goal that caught Alex Stepney unawares — it had been a quiet game so far for the Manchester United custodian. But then it was Denis Law's turn to shine. The first came from the penalty spot; the second from an inch-perfect George Best cross.

There was style about this Manchester United team, but there was also grim determination, personified on this occasion by Bill Foulkes, a

DID YOU KNOW?
West Ham's goal scorer this day, John 'Charlo' Charles, made history as the first black man to play for the club. He was the elder brother of Clive Charles, who played for West Ham and Cardiff City in the 1970s and went on to coach the United States national team. Sadly, both brothers recently died of cancer.

Manchester United fans invade the field to celebrate their team's 1967 League Championship win.

THE RESULT

	WEST HAM UNITED	MANCHESTER UNITED
ATTENDANCE 38,424	**1** Charles	**6** Charlton, Crerand, Foulkes, Best, Law (2, 1 pen)

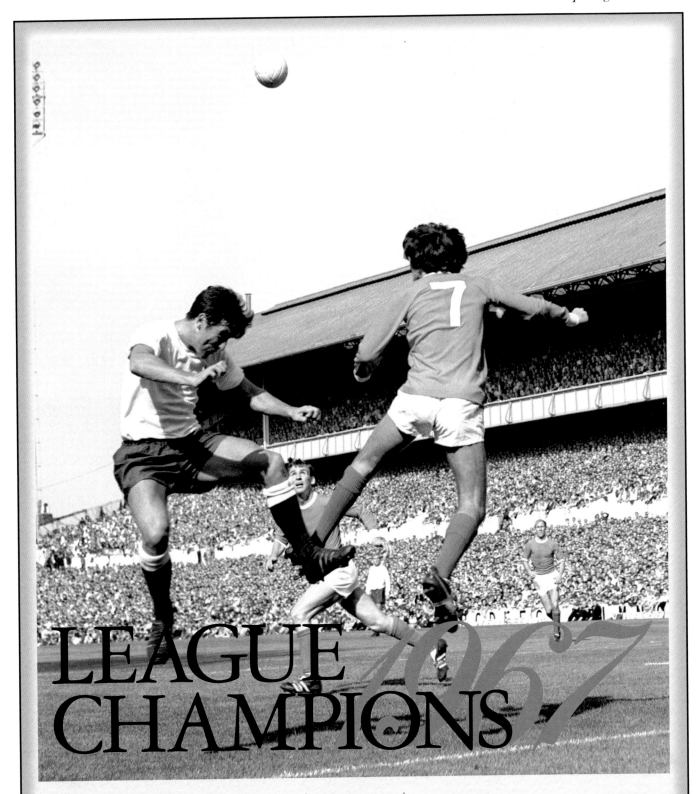

LEAGUE CHAMPIONS 1967

As there had been in 1965, and indeed 1966, there were again a number of clubs capable of mounting a serious challenge for the 1967 League Championship title. Everton had made their intent clear by signing England's Alan Ball from Blackpool for £110,000 – the first six-figure transfer fee between English clubs. Tottenham Hotspur had paid Blackburn Rovers £95,000 for the services of the Welsh international centre half Mike England, and the North London club had also signed Terry Venables from Chelsea for £80,000. Leeds United were still strong and there was always a chance of

George Best heads the ball away from Tottenham Hotspur's Terry Venables. Following wins in 1908, 1911, 1952, 1956, 1957 and 1965, this was Manchester United's seventh League title, equalling the record jointly held at that time by Arsenal and Liverpool.

a team coming from nowhere – this season that team would turn out to be Nottingham Forest.

Chelsea too made their mark early with a good 2-1 win over West Ham United at Upton Park but, ominously, it was Manchester United who made the brightest start with a 5-3 win over West Bromwich Albion at Old Trafford, with two goals from Denis Law and one each from Best, David Herd and Nobby Stiles.

Two more goals from the Lawman earned a midweek win over Everton at Goodison Park but then the Reds were brought down with a crash the following Saturday when George's goal wasn't enough to prevent a 3-1 defeat at Elland ➤

> *"If the Championship were decided on home games we would win it every season. This time our away games made the difference. We got into the right frame of mind."* **George Best**

➤ Road. The 1966/67 League Championship race would turn out to be quite a battle.

In mid-September, Blackpool registered a 5-1 League Cup win over Manchester United at Bloomfield Road, but in the League, Denis Law was on fire and as the autumn went on Manchester United started grinding out results and cementing their position among the leading pack.

RECORD ATTENDANCES

Attendances hit record highs at Old Trafford this season and there was always a boost in ticket sales whenever they played away. And, six years after the maximum wage was abolished, players' wages were also going up, though not as fast at Old Trafford as they were elsewhere – Matt Busby still thought that £4,000 a year was quite enough for any footballer.

Brian Kidd was the latest star of the youth team and David Herd scored 16 times in the League, despite spending the second half the season on the treatment table. But it was still Charlton, Law and Best who stole most of the headlines as Manchester United eventually took

DID YOU KNOW?

It was Queen's Park Rangers who went on to win the League Cup in 1967. The West London outfit were inspired by a young forward by the name of Rodney Marsh, with whom George Best would later famously join forces at Fulham.

the League title with a four-point margin from their nearest rivals.

CELTIC: CHAMPIONS OF EUROPE

Meanwhile, north of the border, Jock Stein's Glasgow Celtic became the first British side to win the European Cup after a 2-1 victory over Inter Milan in the final at the National Stadium in Lisbon. It was Tommy Gemmell who was arguably the greatest hero of the night: the left back scored the equalizer after half time and then set up the winner for Steve Chalmers. Gemmell, a world class player and a regular for a very good Scottish international side, would come up against George Best the following season in the Home Internationals, as we shall see... *Sporting*LEGENDS

LEAGUE DIVISION ONE 1966/1967 FINAL TABLE							
	P	W	D	L	F	A	PTS
Manchester United	42	24	12	6	84	45	60
Nottingham Forest	42	23	10	9	64	41	56
Tottenham Hotspur	42	24	8	10	71	48	56

Manchester United manager Matt Busby holds the League Championship trophy aloft as he and his players parade it around Old Trafford: (left-right) Nobby Stiles, David Sadler (arms raised), Shay Brennan, John Aston, Denis Law (hidden), Bobby Charlton, Busby, Alex Stepney, Pat Crerand, George Best, Jimmy Ryan and Tony Dunne.

© Colorsport

1967-1968

With two League Championship medals already, and still only 21 years old, George Best embarks on the most celebrated season of his career.

*Sporting*LEGENDS
George Best Match Programme 1967-1968

IRELAND
VS
SCOTLAND

WINDSOR PARK
BELFAST
Date **21 October 1967**
Kick-off **3pm**

HOME INTERNATIONAL

Jennings

McKeag   Stewart   Neill   Parke

Campbell   Clements   Nicholson   Best

Crossan   Dougan

McCalliog

Law   Grieg   Wallace

Morgan   Murdoch   Gemmell

McCreadie   Ure   McKinnon

Simpson

HOME INTERNATIONAL
Northern Ireland
VS
Scotland

VENUE	Windsor Park
DATE	Saturday, 21 October 1967
KICK-OFF	3pm

That European Cup quarter final match against Benfica the year before may have been the best George Best performance Bobby Charlton ever saw but many observers, George's father included, would rate this Home International against Scotland as his finest moment. This wasn't a great team performance inspired by one man – Glentoran's Arthur Stewart made his mark but some of his more illustrious team mates (Derek Dougan, for example) did not play particularly well – this was a one-man show.

There were already a number of voices, most notably in the Belfast press, who were suggesting that their star player was not showing anything like the same commitment to his country as he did to his club, so George felt he had something to prove to his countrymen.

The 1967 Home International Championship was decided at Wembley, where the World Cup holders England faced Scotland on 15 April. England needed only a draw to win the title. Scotland won 3-2 and promptly declared themselves World Champions!

An early shot from thirty yards stings Ronnie Simpson's hands; then he goes past two or three players before cutting inside and delivering a right-footed cross that Derek Dougan can't quite get to. "On another day," said George, "I might have scored three or four myself but their goalkeeper Ronnie Simpson, who was only winning his third cap, played a blinder. He was unbelievable. I was hitting shots that were flying towards the top corner and he was suddenly appearing from nowhere to tip them over."

TEAM GAME
Pat Crerand uses the word 'torture' to describe what George did to Tommy Gemmell. Wearing the famous number 11 and playing on the left wing, George gave Gemmell such a hard time in the first half that during the changeover the Celtic full back asked Eddie McCreadie if he'd be so kind as to switch flanks for the second half. McCreadie's reply was abrupt and forthright – he'd seen this sort of thing before and there was no way he was getting involved with George on this kind ➤

"This was my game for Belfast, showing them, perhaps for the only time, what the boy from Burren Way could do when the mood took him. People there still talk about it as the greatest individual performance in an international." **George Best**

THE OPPOSITION

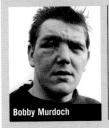
Bobby Murdoch

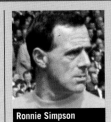
Ronnie Simpson

Tommy Gemmell

BOASTING FOUR of the Celtic team that had just won the European Cup – Ronnie Simpson, Tommy Gemmell, Bobby Murdoch and Willie Wallace – Scotland were more than capable of holding their own against anybody. Under normal circumstances they would have fancied their chances of coming away from Windsor Park with a result against a Northern Ireland team that, without George's services, had just managed a 0-0 draw with Wales. But these were not normal circumstances.

© Mirrorpix

"He caused as much trouble as three men with some exhilarating runs and shots of quite remarkable force from such a slight frame." The Times

➤ of form. It might have been a team game but this time Gemmell was on his own.

It was a remarkable performance. Scotland were a good side, but there are times when it looks like George is playing against kids. It's like the games he used to play on the Cregagh Estate – they come at him in their twos and threes but he keeps tackling back and insisting that the ball is his; they can't get it off him.

They still call this game the 'George Best international' – and if Ronnie Simpson hadn't been on such fine form, the score line could easily have been more convincing.

The goal was scored by Dave Clements of Coventry City, but it was set up by George Best. Playing and receiving a one-two from John Parke, George sets off, this time down the right wing. He has Bobby Murdoch covering him, but you can see that Murdoch knows he cannot dare to try to make a tackle, that if he so much as moves for the ball he will be humiliated by a swerve or a dummy, or a sudden burst of acceleration. Murdoch just has to stay there and make it look

like he's doing his job. Mercifully, he doesn't have to stay there long: George whips in a perfect low cross that bounces off a defender; Clements controls the ball well and strikes it past Simpson for the winner.

"I'LL HAVE IT!"

There were only 20 minutes left to play and Northern Ireland should have been keen to close the game down and grind out the win. Indeed, Pat Jennings looks like he's happy to do that, but George still wants to play football. Terry Neil remembers Jennings holding onto the ball and

Unfortunately for Scotland, on 21 October 1967 George Best felt he had something to prove for Northern Ireland. He didn't play often enough in a green shirt but this performance gave his countrymen something they would never forget.

obviously contemplating hoofing it long and into touch, to waste a few more seconds. But then he hears George: "I'll have it! I'll have it!" As usual, there was much more running left in those legs than anyone else had; much more appetite for the game. Just like he used to stay out after dark in Cregagh, playing on when all the other kids had gone home, the win wasn't enough – he just wanted to play football.

"Everybody that was there on the day called it the George Best game," says Pat Jennings. "And there were Scottish players with big, big reputations in that team. And he was just walking past people on the day. That will be the game to remember him for." *Sporting*LEGENDS

THE RESULT

NORTHERN IRELAND	SCOTLAND
1	**0**
Clements	ATTENDANCE 55,000

REAL MADRID

Sporting **LEGENDS**

1967-1968

GEORGE BEST MATCH PROGRAMME

MANCHESTER UNITED

Date **15 May 1968**
Venue **Estadio Santiago Bernabeu**
Kick-off **9pm**

EUROPEAN CUP SEMI FINAL SECOND LEG

Betancourt

Zoco

Sanchís

González

Sunzunegui

Pérez

Gento

Pirri

Grosso

Velázquez

Amancio

Best

Kidd

Crerand

Stiles

Charlton

Aston

Brennan

Dunne

Sadler

Foulkes

Stepney

EUROPEAN CUP SEMI FINAL SECOND LEG

Real Madrid
VS
Manchester United

VENUE	Estadio Santiago Bernabeu
DATE	Wednesday, 15 May 1968
KICK-OFF	9pm

Arriving in Manchester for the first leg of this European Cup semi final without their star forward Amancio, Real Madrid had played an uncharacteristically defensive game at Old Trafford. Eschewing their usual attacking football for a cagey approach, it was left to the home side to make all the running. The only goal of that first game had come from the boot of George Best – Brian Kidd's long pass had found Aston on the left and Aston had got to the byeline before cutting inside and crossing for Best, who hit a thunderous left-footed shot that gave Betancourt no chance.

The home side had chances to improve upon their lead: Aston was denied by Betancourt after receiving the ball from a Best cross, and from the resulting corner Crerand hit the post; then Brian Kidd should have doubled the advantage for the second leg but he hit the ball high into the Stretford End after a lovely team move. In the end, that slender one-goal advantage would be all Matt Busby's team would take to the second leg three weeks later.

He played in the centre of midfield for England, but at club level Nobby Stiles was a centre back. On this occasion, however, Matt Busby pushed him forward into midfield to man-mark Amancio, while David Sadler began the game alongside Bill Foulkes at the heart of the Manchester United defence.

ATTACKING FLAIR

Now, on a hot night in Madrid, with Amancio back for the home side and with their own star striker Denis Law missing from the team through injury, it was Manchester United's turn to defend as the reigning Spanish champions came out of their shell and played with all the attacking flair that had made them famous the world over. Their forward line of Amancio, Grosso, Velázquez and Pérez kept the Reds in their own half but somehow Manchester United held out for half an hour.

Eventually, however, the home side took the lead when Amancio's free kick was headed home by Pirri. Then, suddenly, it was 2-0 on the night when Gento beat Brennan to a long pass ➤

👁 EYEWITNESS **What the manager said...**

"Don't give up hope! Remember: the score isn't 3-1 for Real Madrid, because George scored at Old Trafford. You're only 3-2 down overall at the moment; there's just a single goal in it. Time to attack!" **Matt Busby**

THE OPPOSITION

Amancio

THE MIGHTY Real Madrid were already chasing their seventh European Cup victory. The Spanish giants had won the trophy for the first five years of its existence – from 1956 to 1960 – and had triumphed again in the 1966

final with a 2-1 win over Partizan Belgrade of Yugoslavia. They had also been beaten finalists in 1962 and 1964. They may not have been quite the team they had been in the 1950s but their European Cup

Betancourt

pedigree was unrivalled and Matt Busby still rated them as a better side than either Juventus or Benfica, the two other giants of the European game who had been drawn to play each other in the other semi final.

Gento

Manchester United pose before their semi-final match against Real Madrid at the Bernabeu. Back row: Stiles, Crerand, Brennan, Stepney, Charlton and Foulkes. Front row: Dunne, Kidd, Sadler, Best and Aston.

OFF THE PITCH Number 1
13 May 1968

🇬🇧 Louis Armstrong
What A Wonderful World
🇺🇸 Archie Bell & The Drells
Tighten Up

"We'd been having a tussle all through the game," said George. "But with time running out I knew I had to try to make it count whenever I got possession. I drew Sanchís towards the tackle but he was too clever to lunge in, jockeying for position and trying to nudge me towards the line and out of the danger zone. I feinted to go inside but then took the ball past him on the outside, relying on my speed to get a yard or two of space to make the cross.

BIG BILL FOULKES
"Big Bill Foulkes had charged out of defence and was the nearest man. God knows what had got into him because it was totally out of character, and everyone on the bench was screaming at him to get back where he belonged. Anyway, Bill was there so I gave him the ball. As I did so I thought: here we go… In training, whenever Bill had a shot he always blasted it over the bar, and I was sure this one was going to go into the stand.

"What happened amazed us all. Coming in at

> *"A lot of people thought we wouldn't do it, but my mind kept going back to Benfica two years earlier when we had a one-goal lead from the first leg and went out there and scored five. If we could do it once, we could do it again."* **George Best**

➤ from Pirri and drove the ball home. Manchester United scored a vital away goal when a long shot from Dunne went into the net off Zoco, but then Amancio pounced to give Real Madrid a 3-1 lead by half time.

TACTICAL CHANGE
At half time Matt Busby made a critical tactical change that would alter the course of the tie. Dave Sadler, who had been playing at centre back alongside Bill Foulkes, was pushed up into attack with George Best and Brian Kidd as Manchester United switched to a 4-3-3. The change took Real Madrid by surprise.

Sadler it was who nipped in to put his side level on aggregate after a Crerand free kick was headed on by Foulkes. Then, with 12 minutes left to play, Crerand took a throw in on the right and gave the ball to George, who found himself up against Manolo Sanchís – not for the first time that night.

DID YOU KNOW?
Defensive stalwart Bill Foulkes, by now 36 years old, was a member of the Manchester United team that had been knocked out of the European Cup by Real Madrid at the semi final stage back in 1957.

the far post, Bill calmly sidefooted the ball into the corner of the net. I couldn't have done it better myself."

The final ten minutes were played out almost entirely in Manchester United's half, but they held out for the draw they needed on the night.

A 2-1 home defeat by Sunderland four days earlier had cost them their League title but now they were playing for even higher stakes: Manchester United, once again inspired by the brilliance of George Best, were through to the European Cup final. *Sporting*LEGENDS

THE RESULT

REAL MADRID	MANCHESTER UNITED	
3	**3**	ATTENDANCE 125,000
Pirri, Gento, Amancio	Zoco (og), Sadler, Foulkes	

Sporting LEGENDS

GEORGE BEST
IN PICTURES

Playing at Highbury in 1968. The
Arsenal defender in the background
is Frank McClintock.

Posing for a Manchester United
press shot in 1969.

Representing his country against
England in the 1971 Home
Internationals.

GEORGE BEST
IN PICTURES

At Old Trafford on 18 September
1971 – the day he scored a hat trick
against West Ham.

Showing off his juggling skills for
the benefit of the photographers.

SportingLEGENDS
GEORGE BEST
IN PICTURES

Posing for another Manchester
United press shot in 1971 – the
beard has yet to take over.

Playing for Northern Ireland in a
World Cup qualifier in 1976.

Sporting LEGENDS
1967-1968

GEORGE BEST MATCH PROGRAMME

MANCHESTER UNITED
vs
BENFICA

Date **29 May 1968**   Venue **Wembley Stadium**   Kick-off **7.45pm**

EUROPEAN CUP FINAL

Stepney

Foulkes   Stiles   Dunne

Brennan   Aston

Sadler   Charlton

Crerand

Best   Kidd

Torres   Eusebio

Augusto

Coluna   Graça

Simoes   Adolfo

Jacinto   Humberto

Cruz

Hennrique

EUROPEAN CUP FINAL

Manchester United
VS
Benfica

VENUE	Wembley Stadium
DATE	Wednesday, 29 May 1968
KICK-OFF	8pm

Having disposed of Real Madrid in the semi final, Manchester United were favourites to win the trophy at Wembley. Indeed, for Pat Crerand, there could only be one winner: "Before the game I was never so sure in my life about winning the game. I thought we were a certainty."

But despite Crerand's confidence, this was no forgone conclusion: Manchester United were still without the injured Denis Law, so the onus would fall squarely on George's slender shoulders to be, as Alex Stepney put it, "the kingpin on the night". But even as Bobby Charlton and Mario Coluna exchanged pennants in the centre circle before the kick off, George's part in the game had been written by Benfica manager Otto Gloria.

"First Cruz tried to stop me," George recalled. "Then it was Humberto's turn. Eusebio struck the bar and although Aston was getting plenty of joy on the other flank, it was a thoughtful dressing room at half time as Busby set to work trying to lift us during the ten-minute break."

HOT, HUMID NIGHT
It was a hot, humid night and even if he hadn't been as closely marked as he was, the notoriously energy-sapping Wembley turf was not suited for

Below: Bobby Charlton (left) scores the opening goal past Benfica goalkeeper José Henrique.

his brand of individualism. George would have to wait until everyone else had run themselves into the ground before he would get the chance to really make his mark on the game.

Even without much influence from the man who had by now become the undisputed star of the team, it was the English side who eventually broke the deadlock after 55 minutes: out on the left wing, Dunne played the ball for Sadler; Sadler cut inside onto his favoured right foot and from the edge of the box, crossed for Charlton, who was running across the face of the goal but somehow managed a deftly flicked header that looped ➤

THE OPPOSITION

Torres

OF ALL THE GREAT European sides of the 1960s, Benfica had perhaps the advantage of already knowing first hand just what George Best could do. The defeat he

Graça

had inspired in 1966 was still fresh in the memory and Otto Gloria knew that he would have to deploy spoiling tactics if his team were to contain the Manchester United

winger at Wembley. "Of the United players," the Benfica manager said before the game, "the one I especially admire is Best – he is how we say muito bon."

Eusebio

George Best scores Manchester United's second goal.

Left: Benfica 1968. Cruz, Humberto, Graça, Jacinto, Adolfo, Henrique; Augusto, Torres, Eusebio, Coluna, Simões.

Below left: Nobby Stiles gets involved with José Torres (4th left) after a foul on Crerand, who lies motionless.

DID YOU KNOW?

Sarajevo had already tried to kick George out of the game in the second round – the Yugoslavians were, in Pat Crerand's words, a "tough, tough" team. But George's only response to their kicking and scare tactics was to score the goal that sent Manchester United through to the third round.

➤ over Henrique and into the back of the net. It was his first headed goal in a long time and one that Denis Law would have been proud of. Manchester United were ahead.

Benfica were not a side to fall apart on the big occasion, however, and they got their reward for staying in the fight ten minutes from time: Torres won a header in the penalty area and the ball bounced out wide, beyond Eusebio, for Jaime Graça who, from the tightest of angles, got his right foot high above the ball and drilled it low across Stepney for the equalizer.

GOALKEEPING HEROICS

Benfica could even have won it at the death: Eusebio beat Nobby Stiles, Bill Foulkes and then Tony Dunne, before letting go a rocket that looked destined for the net, but which instead landed square in the middle of Stepney's chest and somehow stuck. Eusebio came rushing in for the rebound, but it never came out to him and the Mozambiquean was left to wait for Stepney to clear the ball before sportingly congratulating him on what would eventually turn out to be the match-winning save.

Alex Stepney describes how George conjured up the winner in extra time. "After the 90 minutes it was 1-1. These lads were absolutely shattered. It was 100,000 in there; it was 90 degrees, and they now know they've got to go and do another 30 minutes of extra time.

"We kicked off and the ball came back to me. I gave it to Tony Dunne; Tony Dunne gave it back to me. I gave it to Shay Brennan and he gave it back to me. No one wanted the ball off me and I thought: I've got to kick it down, which is not what I'd usually have done."

SUPERIOR FITNESS

And that's where George's superior fitness came

Below right: Matt Busby (centre right) and his assistant Jimmy Murphy (left, leaning) try to inspire their players before the start of extra time.

into play. He was the only one on the pitch who still had any running left in him. Brian Kidd flicked Stepney's ball on and there was George.

"George was off," recalls Charlton, "giving a fair impression of Wembley's electric hare, supremely confident, doing ultimately what he always expected of himself in such situations. When George got away like that goalkeepers were inclined to feel they had chosen the wrong career, and I'm sure Henrique was no exception." George beat Coluna to the ball just outside the penalty area, walked past Coluna, walked past Henrique as the goalkeeper came out to close him down ➤

👁 EYEWITNESS What the players said…

"I think the game was disappointing from his point of view. George loved the big stage and you could hardly get a bigger stage than the European Cup final. I could see in everything he did that he wanted to use it as a platform for a great virtuoso performance, but it didn't quite happen." **Bobby Charlton**

Below left: George signs photos of himself for young fans in a train before leaving London for the post-match reception in Manchester.

⏱OFF THE PITCH
On this day

After three weeks of increasingly violent demonstrations against de Gaulle's government, French prime minister Georges Pompidou sends tanks to the outskirts of Paris to quell the rioting there.

➤ and calmly rolled the ball into the empty net. That was the inspiration Manchester United needed. Soon, birthday boy Brian Kidd had headed home the third and then Charlton made it 4-1 after another clever run towards the near post.

The Manchester United skipper was as modest as always about his achievement: "I literally just helped it on its way," says Sir Bobby. "I knew where the goals were; I knew where the keeper was and I just helped it on its way into the far post. 4-1."

"When the final whistle went," he continues, "the first thing the players did was to go and get the old man. They realised how much it meant to him. When Munich happened he was decimated. This just made it a little bit better for him. But it's something special to be the best, and we were the best." *Sporting*LEGENDS

THE RESULT

MANCHESTER UNITED	BENFICA	(1-1 FT)
4	**1** AET	
Charlton (2), Best, Kidd	Torres	ATTENDANCE 100,000

José Henrique races out of his goal to challenge George Best.

George and Bobby
celebrate their victory.

EUROPEAN CHAMPIONS *1968*

" I am the proudest man in England tonight. The boys have done us proud. They showed in Madrid that they have the heart to fight back and tonight they showed us the stuff that Manchester United are made of. " **Matt Busby**

For Matt Busby, who would receive a knighthood in June, it was the culmination of a life's work; for Bobby Charlton, it was the gift he would leave for the friends he had lost in the Munich air disaster ten years earlier; for Bill Foulkes it was the crowning achievement of an outstanding career. For George Best it was, or should have been, just the beginning.

Right: Pat Crerand, George Best and Matt Busby celebrate with the European Cup, the day after their 4-1 win over Benfica.

He had been Manchester United's top scorer in the League with 28 goals that season and his reputation now spread far beyond Britain – and also far beyond football.

WARM GLOW OF EXPECTANCY

"I thought nothing other than that everything was in front of me, and that our achievements would be limitless," he wrote in his final book, *Hard Tackles and Dirty Baths*. "We had such a formidable side, and everything was set up at the club for true greatness. You could sense something special. I had never known disappointment from day one in football. Life could not have been sweeter. The warm glow of expectancy could not have been greater."

Winning the European Cup may have been Sir Matt Busby's greatest moment and Manchester United's finest achievement to date but, though he didn't realise it at the time, and wouldn't for a long time, for George it was the beginning of the end. Sir Matt Busby was once asked when exactly he thought George's career started to go downhill. "As soon as he got to the top," the manager replied, after no more than a moment's thought.

It would be some time yet before the off-field distractions that would eventually destroy his career would begin to show their effects – and there would still be plenty more magnificent performances from him before that happened – but it is telling that when George asked himself what he could remember about the night's celebrations after that victory, he found he couldn't recall a single incident. *Sporting*LEGENDS

ROAD TO WEMBLEY

First round (*of Malta)		
20 Sept 1967 **Hibernians***	(H) **4-0** Law (2), Sadler (2)	
27 Sept 1967 **Hibernians***	(A) **0-0**	
Aggregate **4-0**		
Second round		
15 Nov 1967 **Sarajevo**	(A) **0-0**	
29 Nov 1967 **Sarajevo**	(H) **2-1** Aston, Best	
Aggregate **2-1**		
Quarter final		
28 Feb 1968 **Gornik Zabrze**	(H) **2-0** Kidd, og	
13 Mar 1968 **Gornik Zabrze**	(A) **0-1**	
Aggregate **2-1**		
Semi final		
24 April 1968 **Real Madrid**	(H) **1-0** Best	
15 May 1968 **Real Madrid**	(A) **3-3** og, Sadler, Foulkes	
Aggregate **4-3**		
Final (**Wembley)		
29 May 1968 **Benfica**	** **4-1** Charlton (2), Best, Kidd	

DID YOU KNOW?

Because Manchester City won the League in 1968, the 1968/69 European Cup included two representatives from Manchester. Unfortunately, City went out to Fenerbahce in the first round, while United got as far as the semi final before losing 2-1 on aggregate to eventual winners AC Milan.

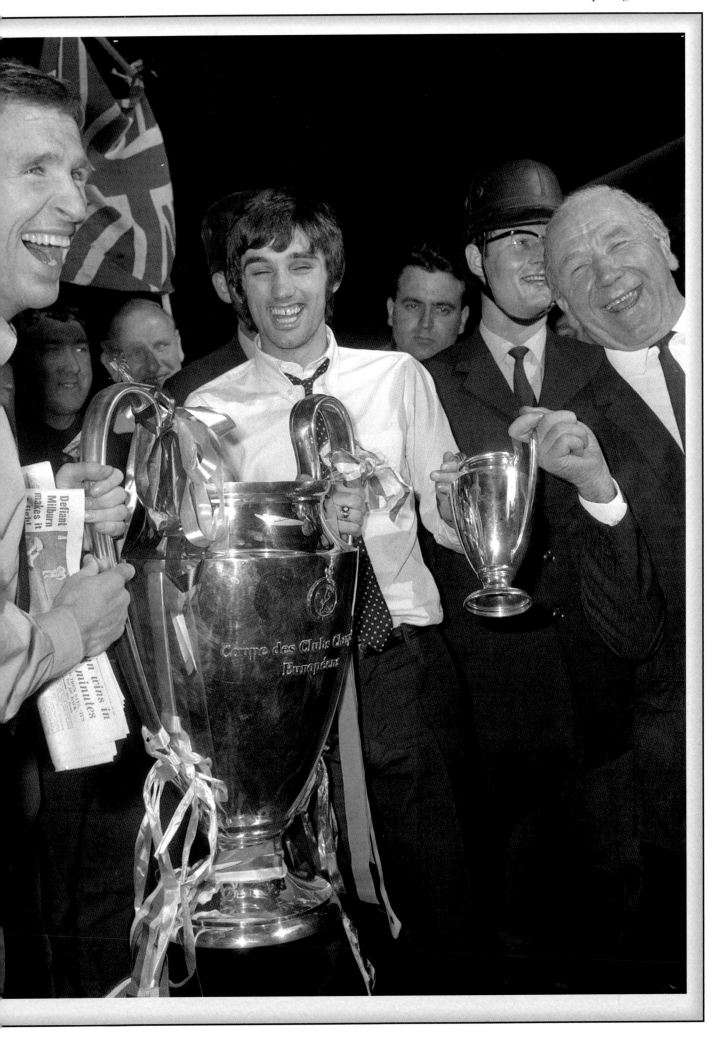

PLAYER OF THE YEAR

" At twenty-two, I had already won everything. For the next ten years I thought I would be at the top of my game with the best club in the world, winning trophy after trophy, season after season. It is hard to believe that, within four years, it would all go horribly wrong." **George Best**

Twice a League champion and now a European champion, George Best had become the most famous football player in the world.

Sir Stanley Matthews, Ferenc Puskas and Alfredo di Stéfano were fast-retreating memories; Eusebio, the outstanding player of the 1966 World Cup, had just been upstaged by George in a European Cup final; Cruyff was still a boy and even Pelé was not as famous as he would become in the summer of 1970. And none of them ever achieved quite the public profile that George had in 1968.

SWINGING SIXTIES

George Best had become the face of the swinging sixties and was certainly living up to his reputation as the 'Fifth Beatle'. Until George Best, all athletes wore their hair short; all football players (except Denis Law) wore their shirts tucked neatly into their shorts; and all young boys thought that a career in football could never bring anything more than glory on the field of play. George changed all that.

His basic wage at Manchester United may not have been that much compared to the super-

DID YOU KNOW?
George had even been asked to advertise Playtex bras. He had to walk into a bar, see a girl and offer to buy her a drink. She was able to refuse because if you're wearing a Playtex bra you can turn down even Britain's most eligible bachelor.

BRITISH FOOTBALLER OF THE YEAR '64–'68
'64 Bobby Moore
'65 Bobby Collins
'66 Bobby Charlton
'67 Jack Charlton
'68 George Best

EUROPEAN PLAYER OF THE YEAR '64–'68
'64 Denis Law
'65 Eusebio
'66 Bobby Charlton
'67 Florian Albert
'68 George Best

inflated wages of today's top players – though it was certainly a lot more than most people were earning – but he was earning very good bonuses and an awful lot of money from his interests outside the game, notably his modelling and advertising, rather than his often ill-founded business ventures. He had more money than he knew what to do with, and more than enough to be able to go out and buy an E-type Jaguar for cash any time he felt like it.

GREY SKIES AND BAD FOOD

Despite the assurances of Harold Macmillan a decade before, however, Britain had largely remained a country of grey skies and bad food. For so many people, the only relief from the gloom was the sight of George Best running down the wing with his long hair and shirt hanging out.

But by 1968, England had suddenly become the coolest country on the planet. The Beatles were the biggest rock band in the world, the Rolling Stones were the second biggest band in the world, the British film industry was booming, Manchester United were European champions – and all the talk in the taprooms was about Georgie Best. *Sporting*LEGENDS

1968-1970

Being the most famous football player on the planet brings unwanted attention; from the press, from the fans, and often from opposing defenders.

*Sporting*LEGENDS

GEORGE BEST
MATCH
PROGRAMME
1968-1969

Date **26 February 1969**
Venue **Old Trafford**
Kick-off **7.45pm**

**MANCHESTER
UNITED
VS
RAPID
VIENNA**

EUROPEAN CUP QUARTER FINAL FIRST LEG

Stepney

Dunne

Stiles

Fitzpatrick   James   Best

Charlton

Morgan   Crerand

Kidd

Law

●

Kaltenbrunner

Grausam

Flögel   Bjerregaard

Söndergaard   Fritsch   Gebhardt

Fak   Ullmann

Glechner

Fuchsbichler

EUROPEAN CUP QUARTER FINAL FIRST LEG

Manchester United
VS
Rapid Vienna

VENUE	Old Trafford
DATE	Wednesday, 26 February 1969
KICK-OFF	7.45pm

Having knocked out Waterford and Anderlecht, Manchester United now faced a sterner test in their bid to retain the European Cup. The Irish part-timers had been beaten 3-1 away and 7-1 at home, with Denis Law scoring a hat trick in Waterford and four goals in the second leg at Old Trafford; Anderlecht were beaten 3-0 at home, with Denis Law again scoring twice, though it still took an away goal from Carlo Sartori in Belgium to take the holders through as Anderlecht gave Sir Matt Busby's side a real scare by winning the second leg 3-1.

However, though they had managed to get through to the quarter finals of the European Cup, and though they may have even started fancying their chances of emulating Benfica and Inter Milan by retaining the trophy (even if there was still some way to go before they could consider themselves to be in the same category as Real Madrid, and there still is) it was slowly becoming apparent that not all was well at Old Trafford.

ERRATIC FORM
Manchester United's League form had been erratic all season. They had started well enough with a 2-1 home win over Everton but would go on from

DID YOU KNOW?
It was around about this time that George, who was earning a very healthy basic wage of £700 a week, discovered that Charlton and Law were both on twice that much money.

there to win only three of their first nine League games, before becoming progressively distracted by their European Cup exploits. They would end the 1968/69 League campaign in 11th place, having won 15 and lost 15 of their 42 matches.

FA CUP REPLAY
The FA Cup was proving to be a bit of a struggle too. After beating Exeter City 3-1 at St James Park, they had needed a replay to overcome Watford in the fourth round and another to beat Birmingham City in the fifth round.

And that was the problem: that FA Cup replay had been scheduled for the Monday before this vital European match. Although a Denis Law hat trick had helped Manchester United to a convincing 6-2 victory, the mere fact that tonight's match came just two days later gave Rudolf Vytlacil's side what he considered to be an advantage: ➤

👁 EYEWITNESS **What the players said...**

"Success in Europe had become a crusade which dominated everything, and because we were getting through the rounds, everything else got pushed to one side." **Dave Sadler**

THE OPPOSITION

Fritsch

IN THIS, their sixth European Cup campaign, Rapid Vienna had overcome Real Madrid on the newly introduced away goals rule to reach this quarter final

Fuchsbichler

encounter with the holders. In fact, Rapid had come up against the Spanish side before – in 1956/57 when, after losing 4-2 in Madrid, they had won 3-1 in Vienna

to force a play-off against that season's eventual winners. They had also reached the semi finals of the competition in 1961 before losing to the eventual winners

that season, Benfica. Boasting a number of seasoned internationals, they had gone into the winter break comfortably top of the Austrian League.

"It is questionable whether Manchester are capable of repeating such a performance only 48 hours later," the Rapid Vienna coach was bold enough to predict. "It is a long time since I have seen a team in such a physical and mental state of perfection, but we shall not allow United as much room to play as did Birmingham."

COMFORTABLE WINNERS

But tonight there would be no signs of the troubles to come as Manchester United, inspired by George Best, ran out comfortable winners against a team with real European pedigree. It may have helped that there had recently been a

George Best (11) and Denis Law (10) challenge Rapid goalkeeper Gerald Fuchsbichler.

spate of cold weather and a number of games had been postponed. After the game Vytlacil was moved to say what everyone else already knew: "George Best is the top player in all Europe."

But what Vytlacil couldn't have known – what nobody would have even have guessed at the time – was that George had just made his last significant contribution to a European club match. Manchester United would earn a 0-0 draw in Vienna to take them through to the semi finals, but there they would be beaten 2-1 on aggregate by AC Milan. And they would not qualify for Europe again during George's time at the club. In fact, even with George Best, the team was starting

Above: Bobby Charlton unleashes a ferocious shot at the Rapid goal.

Right: George Best in action.

on a slippery slope that would end in their relegation in 1974.

ANTI-CLIMAX

"After the [1968 European Cup final] I felt an anti-climax because it was all over," George reminisced as he tried later in his life to understand what had gone wrong.

"The following couple of seasons became even more of an anti-climax because the team was on the slide. It should have kept going. We should have done a Liverpool; we should have kept winning trophies, and we didn't. We did the opposite." *Sporting*LEGENDS

THE RESULT

MANCHESTER UNITED	RAPID VIENNA	
3	**0**	ATTENDANCE
Best (2), Morgan		61,932

The long, lonely walk

SENT OFF!

Above: George (8) is booked by John Hamewood after colliding with Manchester City's Glyn Pardoe during a Division One match at Old Trafford.

Left: George leaves the field during an international match between Scotland and Northern Ireland in Belfast. He was sent off for throwing mud and spitting at the referee.

As George became increasingly disillusioned with his footballing life – and also as he started becoming more and more distracted by the excesses of his superstar lifestyle – the effects began to show in his disciplinary record. Perhaps the least savoury incident occurred on 18 April 1970 when he was dismissed while playing for Northern Ireland against Scotland in Belfast. The offence: throwing mud and spitting at the referee, without too much provocation. In fairness, he was later spared of any further disciplinary charges for the offence when the International Committee accepted his claim that he had spat at the ground and that the mud-throwing was nothing more than a petulant underhand lob, and not quite how Eric Jennings had described it in his initial report.

But George's reputation went before him and players who did not have the guile or pace of Paul Reaney were often compelled to use more basic tactics to thwart him. Actually, George once said that he only started wearing shinpads when he came up against Paul Reaney, though there might be more to the story than that: it's certainly true that the Leeds United defender was one of the few full backs who ever had the better of George when he was in his prime.

It is amazing that a player who came in for so much attention from defenders was not sent off until 1968. That first dismissal came in the World Club Championship match against Estudiantes on 16 October 1968 when he was ordered from the field of play for fighting with Hugo Medina.

Manchester United had lost the first leg 1-0 in Buenos Aires. In the second leg, Denis Law

> " *Now and again, at completely arbitrary moments, he appears to have an irresistible desire to put two fingers up to the whole world.*" **Hugh McIlvanney**

DID YOU KNOW?
Hugh McIlvanney can remember the days of the Brown Bull pub in Manchester when Georgie Best Superstar used to take orders for fish suppers and then go off and collect them – and get all the orders right.

Above: George is walked off by Tony Dunne and Bobby Charlton after being sent off by referee Norman Burtenshaw.

Left: George with Sir Matt (left) and PFA Secretary Cliff Lloyd (centre) refuting allegations that he deliberately broke Glyn Pardoe's leg.

had to be taken off after a confrontation with the goalkeeper and then a gentleman called Hugo Medina came up. We'll let George explain:

"This guy, Medina, just came up to me and kicked me, no intention of playing the ball, no intention of playing football of any description, just whacked me as hard as he could and spat at me for good measure." Medina was booked, but George couldn't leave it there. He smacked him in the mouth and walked off the pitch towards the changing rooms before the referee even had the chance to point in the general direction.

SUSPENDED

Then, on 2 January 1970, he was sent off again, this time for knocking the ball out of referee Jack Taylor's hands at the end of a League Cup semi final match at Maine Road. For that he was fined £100 and suspended for four weeks. He would come back from suspension just in time for the FA Cup fifth round match at Northampton Town, which, if you're a Cobblers fan, was probably a week too early... *Sporting*LEGENDS

Sporting **LEGENDS**

GEORGE BEST MATCH PROGRAMME

1969-1970

NORTHAMPTON TOWN vs MANCHESTER UNITED

Date 7 February 1970 Venue The County Ground Kick-off 3pm

FA CUP FIFTH ROUND

Book

Brookes   Clarke   Rankmore   Fairfax

Fairbrother   Kiernan   Ross   Felton

Large   McNeil

Best   Kidd

Sartori   Charlton   Crerand   Morgan

Dunne   Sadler   Ure   Edwards

Stepney

FA CUP FIFTH ROUND

Northampton Town
VS
Manchester United

VENUE	The County Ground
DATE	Saturday, 7 February 1970
KICK-OFF	3pm

"**S**ix of the Best on bad boy's return!" ran one newspaper headline. Even after such a momentous achievement as this double hat trick, the press couldn't bring themselves to enjoy it with him; they had to find a negative slant. What the 'bad boy' had actually done, of course, was to get himself booked during a match against Manchester City and then booked again as he came off the pitch for knocking the ball out of Jack Taylor's hands. It was petulant but it was also almost playful. Either way, it was dissent and it meant a dismissal.

Now, four weeks' suspension for getting booked twice might seem a little harsh by today's standards, and indeed, it was a harsh punishment then, but one didn't argue with the FA and George had paid his £100 fine and sat out his time without a murmur of complaint.

VOCIFEROUS MINORITY

There was by now a vociferous minority, both outside and inside the game – some of them even within the Old Trafford dressing room – who thought that Manchester United were better off without George Best. The facts tell another story: George had already netted 14 goals in all ➤

© Mirrorpix

👁 EYEWITNESS **What the players said...**

"The closest I got to him was when we shook hands at the end of the game." **Roy Fairfax**

THE OPPOSITION

Dixie McNeill

NORTHAMPTON TOWN had been in the First Division until their relegation in 1966 but they were now a Third Division side seriously on the slide. Never the less,

Frank Large

they had reached the fifth round of the FA Cup this year and against a Manchester United side that was experiencing its own difficulties they would have been fancying their

chances. Despite an increase in ticket prices for this game, the County Ground was packed to the rafters for a potential giant killing. But it wasn't to turn out that way.

Kim Book

Above: Northampton Town goalkeeper Kim Book (right) is beaten again by George Best (centre, hidden), for the fourth of his goals.

DID YOU KNOW?

This wasn't the first time a player had scored six goals in an FA Cup tie: Denis Law had managed the remarkable feat for Manchester City against Luton Town in 1961, though that match had to be abandoned with twenty minutes left to play and the records expunged. Luton won the re-match.

➤ competitions before his suspension and was well on the way towards becoming Manchester United's top scorer for the third season running. In fact, he was soon to become something of a one-man band and that band was patently not as good as it had been. The pressure was beginning to tell: he had been turning up for training with the smell of alcohol on his breath after yet another big night out. But he was still young and perfectly able to sweat out the booze on the training pitch. He certainly had no idea that he was developing a drink problem, and it didn't seem to be affecting his game, or his life.

SIX OF THE BEST

This was a majestic return, even against such lowly opposition. The first came from a cross by Brian Kidd and there was George to head the ball home at the far post. The second was a team effort: Sadler to Crerand, and Crerand to Best, who casually sidled past Kim Book to put the ball into the net. For the third, Bobby Charlton passed to Kidd, who gave the ball to George; his first shot is saved but Best is there to lash the rebound home for his hat trick. Brian Kidd sets George up for his fourth before getting onto the score sheet himself. Then George runs onto a through ball from Francis Burns and rolls the ball into the corner of the goal for his fifth and Manchester United's sixth.

HOW MANY?

By now it's just a question of how many. Kidd gets his second of the match before Best finds himself through again. "There's the record!" says the commentator before he has even gone round the keeper Kim Book, who by now is just lying there on the ground watching the ➤

This season, 2005/06, Northampton Town won through to the Third Round of the FA Cup for the third successive season. It is the first time the club has achieved this feat since 1970.

⊘ OFF THE PITCH
On this day
Badfinger play the Carousel Ballroom in Belfast. The band naively turn up with Orange amplifiers, which in those days were all bright orange. "We had this big line-up of orange amps and orange microphones going across stage," recalled a roadie. "We were lucky to get out of there alive."

👁 EYEWITNESS **What the papers said...**

"Best's conduct sheet over a long period is good. Two offences in foreign football and five cautions in domestic competitions is the sum total of his crimes in seven seasons of action in soccer's top grade."

David Meek, Manchester Evening News

© Mirrorpix

➤ proceedings – he doesn't even bother to try to get up any more.

But there are no great celebrations – quite the opposite in fact. George just stands there with his hand on the goalpost, his head bowed, almost embarrassed by what he's just done. Perhaps he didn't dare celebrate for fear of how the media might interpret his actions. Perhaps he knew that if he didn't now press the self-destruct button himself, there were plenty of other people around who would have been more than willing to press it for him. *Sporting*LEGENDS

DID YOU KNOW?

Harold Wilson sent George a telegram to congratulate him on the six goals he scored against Northampton Town. "What is the Prime Minister doing, writing to me?" George asked himself. "It just added to the feeling of unreality."

Right: The match ball, which now resides at the Manchester United Museum.

THE RESULT

NORTHAMPTON TOWN	MANCHESTER UNITED
2	**8**

ATTENDANCE
21,771   McNeill, Large | Best (6), Kidd (2)

Sporting LEGENDS

GEORGE BEST MATCH PROGRAMME

1969-1970

Date **23 March 1970**
Venue **Villa Park**
Kick-off **7.45pm**

MANCHESTER
UNITED
VS
LEEDS
UNITED

FA CUP SEMI FINAL REPLAY

Stepney

Dunne

Stiles

Edwards   Sadler   Sartori

Charlton

Morgan   Crerand

Best

Kidd

Clarke

Jones

Bremner   Lorimer

Giles

Gray   Reaney

Charlton

Cooper   Madeley

Sprake

FA CUP SEMI FINAL REPLAY

Manchester United

VS

Leeds United

VENUE	Villa Park
DATE	Monday, 23 March 1970
KICK-OFF	7.45pm

This was football as it used to be played. There were no penalty shoot-outs, only one substitute allowed and no kicking the ball into touch every time someone broke a fingernail. And it was raining. Heavily. Both before and during the game. George remembered the first match at Hillsborough as "another kicking and punching match", but though this replay was an extremely physical encounter that tested the fitness of all 22 players, it was more mudbath than bloodbath.

Alan Clarke's disallowed goal was the only time the net rippled at either end but this was not, as the score line might suggest, a bruising battle fought in a muddy centre circle: there were chances galore. Manchester United dominated the first half and with a little more luck to match his bravery Brian Kidd would have broken the deadlock. But this Leeds side, marshalled by the incomparable Billy Bremner, was highly resilient and they came out after the break determined to make sure that Alex Stepney earned his money.

ONE OF THE LADS

Neither was the game without incident off the pitch – and that incident involved (surprise, surprise) George, and a female of his acquaintance.

DID YOU KNOW?

This was Manchester United's fourth game in a fortnight, and they would play another four before the month was out. Leeds' fixture list had become so congested that Don Revie would feel he had to field a weakened side in the run-in, a decision that would cost the club both the Championship and a £5,000 fine from the FA.

As the replay was at Villa Park the team had stayed in a hotel in Birmingham, which was where George got into trouble. Wilf McGuinness, who had taken over first-team coaching duties from Sir Matt over the summer, saw it as part of his duty to keep close tabs on the wayward superstar of the side.

Wilf had been with the club for a long time and had always been considered 'one of the lads'. In fact, he was a couple of weeks younger than Bobby Charlton and many of the players had found it difficult to call him 'Boss'. George certainly didn't like being treated 'like a schoolboy' and was beginning to feel that drinking and womanising were not only his prerogative but his duty as a national icon.

Gary Sprake watches the ball flash across his goalmouth. Paul Reaney, Jack Charlton and George Best look on.

THE OPPOSITION

THIS LEEDS UNITED team would become remembered as one of the greatest English sides of all time. They were the current League champions and still very much in the hunt for a unique League, FA Cup and European Cup treble this season. They could dish it out, and they often did, but they could play a bit too. The

Jack Charlton

back four of Paul Reaney, Terry Cooper, Jack Charlton and Paul Madeley were all England internationals; the midfield of Peter Lorimer, Billy Bremner, Johnny Giles and Eddie Gray was as well balanced as it was talented. And in Allan 'Sniffer' Clarke they had one of the finest goal poachers of his generation.

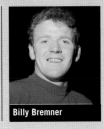

Billy Bremner

Leeds United's Jack Charlton (centre) organizes the defence as Manchester United's Bobby Charlton (9) and George Best (8) hover in the penalty area.

Left: Jack Charlton keeps a close eye on George Best.

⏱ OFF THE PITCH
On this day

Facing a strike by Postal Service workers, US president Richard Nixon declares a state of national emergency.

➤ George had met a girl at the hotel – well, a married woman actually, though that never stopped him – and after one thing had led to another he was late getting onto the coach to leave for the game. Wilf, who'd been aware of developments, was furious and told Sir Matt he was going to send Best straight back to Manchester. Sir Matt calmed his second-in-command down and said they'd sort it out after the game, though in the end, the events of this match would be discipline enough.

NIGHTMARE

George, who remembered the whole 1969/70 campaign as "a horrible season", had a nightmare of a game. The Leeds United players had somehow found out about the incident with the woman at the hotel and decided to try to use it to their advantage by having a go at George about it on the pitch – Johnny Giles was the chief protagonist. It worked. Like the European Cup final at Wembley two years before, the elements again conspired against George's style of play and, try as he might, he just couldn't get into the flow of the game.

Never the less, with another stalemate already looking the most likely outcome, George did have a late chance to win the game for Manchester United. And that was when it all went so horribly wrong for him.

Taking the Leeds United defence and the mud on at the same time, he tried to show off his skills in the atrocious conditions, but even he couldn't contend with the heavy ground as he approached Gary Sprake for the final push. Somehow, the ball got stuck in the mud and George tripped over it, and fell flat on his face. The Leeds fans revelled in his humiliation.

Of course, a lot of people revelled in George Best's humiliation as the trajectory of his career began its descending arc, though at least on this occasion the laughter was good-natured. And it was funny. *Sporting*LEGENDS

Below: George takes on Norman Hunter (right) and Billy Bremner (left).

⊙ OFF THE PITCH Number 1
23 March 1970

🇬🇧 Simon & Garfunkel
Bridge Over Troubled Waters

🇺🇸 Simon & Garfunkel
Bridge Over Troubled Waters

THE RESULT

MANCHESTER UNITED	LEEDS UNITED
0	**0**

ATTENDANCE
62,500

1970-1972

Manchester United are noticeably in decline, though George is still turning in the performances, despite his increasing waywardness off the field of play.

END OF AN ERA

"It looked like the future contained nothing but grafting in the middle of the table, losing as many games as we won." **George Best**

Long after he left the club, George would respectfully opine that perhaps Sir Matt Busby remained loyal to his team for too long. In *Bestie*, Joe Lovejoy's authorized biography of George Best, the author goes so far as to suggest that Sir Matt Busby should have taken his European Cup and his knighthood and retired from the game in the summer of 1968. Sir Matt had turned 59 four days before his team's triumph at Wembley and had fulfilled his life's ambition. It is also true that the only player he signed between 1964 and 1968 was the goalkeeper Alex Stepney.

COMPLACENCY

It was not that the team that won the European Cup was ageing: they were not. Bill Foulkes was 36, Shay Brennan 31, Bobby Charlton 30 and Paddy Crerand 29, but the rest were all 26 ➤

Right: Many people assumed that Sir Matt Busby would retire from management immediately after the European Cup triumph in 1968.

Sir Matt Busby at Old Trafford

Above: Manchester United pose for a team photo with the European Cup.

George with Tommy Docherty

➤ or younger – and Brian Kidd and John Aston were even younger than George Best. The problem was that the team had reached the summit and there were no new players of real quality being brought in to keep them on their toes.

CASE IN POINT

The Scottish winger Willie Morgan was a case in point. Morgan signed for Manchester United from Burnley for £100,000 in the summer of 1968. He had one international cap (from that match against Northern Ireland in 1967) and though he would go on to play 236 games for Manchester United, he would not become a regular with the Scottish team until 1972.

Manchester United, as a club and as a team, were becoming complacent, and it was showing in their results.

"Sometimes he fell a little bit foul, George, not being where he should have been at the right time. But they were incidental little things compared to his contribution to the game generally, which was massive." **Sir Bobby Charlton**

Just as he had become disillusioned with playing for a Northern Ireland team that was never going to compete for honours, so George would soon become disillusioned with Manchester United. He could have moved on – there were plenty of clubs who would have been interested in signing him, including the new League champions Manchester City – but like his mentor, Sir Matt Busby, he loved the club. He really didn't want to play for anyone else.

Indeed, it was Sir Matt who was the first person to come to his bedside after he had contracted deep-vein thrombosis on a flight back from Marbella. "It's about time you were back playing, isn't it?" asked Busby, who still believed that George could turn Manchester United around single-handedly, even though at the time he couldn't even get out of bed.

GOING MISSING

But despite Busby's continued faith in him, George couldn't do anything for his team if he wasn't there. He continued to 'go missing'. He would skip training and be dropped or suspended by the club. He was transfer-listed but nobody came in for him. And there had been more problems off the pitch too: there were driving

Above: George Best turns out for Barry Fry's Dunstable Town in a friendly against Manchester United Reserves at Creasy Park in August 1974.

> **DID YOU KNOW?**
> The Denis Law backheel that won the Manchester derby for City on 27 April 1974 was not the goal that relegated Manchester United: results elsewhere on the day meant that United would have gone down anyway.

offences involving drinking and speeding; there were other court cases involving women, including one in which he was convicted of causing actual bodily harm; there were IRA death threats on two occasions… It had all gone far beyond football and he couldn't take it any more.

The final straw was the altercation with Tommy Docherty. George asserts that his manager reneged on a promise: that if George were to miss training for any reason, he would not be dropped if he came back in for the rest of the week and worked double hard. Such a scenario occurred the week before an FA Cup match with Plymouth Argyle at the start of 1974.

Docherty told George he was dropped. George, outraged at not being considered good enough to play against Argyle, and at what he considered to be a breach of promise, vowed that if he didn't play today he would never play for United again. Docherty wasn't moved. George left the ground. He came back after the game, when everyone else had gone home, to sit in the stands, to soak up the atmosphere and the memories that the ground had given him, to think about what had been and what night have been. Then he left again, and never went back. George Best would never play for Manchester United again. *Sporting*LEGENDS

GEORGE BEST
MATCH
PROGRAMME

Sporting LEGENDS

1970-1971

TOTTENHAM HOTSPUR

vs

MANCHESTER UNITED

Date 5 December 1970 Venue White Hart Lane Kick-off 3pm

FA CUP FIFTH ROUND

Jennings

Kinnear England Beal Knowles

Pearce Mullery Perryman Peters

Gilzean Chivers

Law Kidd

Aston Charlton Fitzpatrick Best

Dunne Sadler James Watson

Rimmer

LEAGUE DIVISION ONE

Tottenham Hotspur
VS
Manchester United

VENUE	White Hart Lane
DATE	Saturday, 5 December 1970
KICK-OFF	3pm

George Best always believed that he could tell how the season was going to turn out for himself and the team by their performance in the opening game. It wasn't necessarily the result that mattered but the way the team played; how the new players fitted in with the exisiting group and how the balance of the side felt.

This season had started with a 1-0 home defeat at the hands of Leeds United, courtesy of a Mick Jones corker. By Christmas, Manchester United were fifth from bottom of the First Division, so a point at White Hart Lane was a good result, but in itself this match is really only notable because it produced George's 100th goal in the League – quite a milestone, certainly, but it was the avalanche of events that occurred after this match that would be of greater importance.

This was to be one of Wilf McGuinness's final matches in charge of the Manchester United first team. After 18 months as manager, which is not very long when you consider that Sir Matt Busby held the post for 24 years, he was relieved of his duties following the 4-4 draw against Derby County at the Baseball Ground on Boxing Day and left the club shortly afterwards under considerable personal stress. Sir Matt took over

until the end of the season, when Leicester City's Frank O'Farrell was appointed. O'Farrell himself would last just eighteen months before being replaced by Tommy Docherty, who would be George's last manager at the club.

RECORD FINE

These behind-the-scenes changes at Manchester United coincided with George's own eventual fall from grace, but for now there were more immediate troubles. January 1971 would be an eventful month, not only in the life of George Best but also for football itself. On 2 January, a staircase collapsed at Ibrox and 66 people ➤

THE OPPOSITION

THIS SPURS side were not the equals of Bill Nicholson's 1961 heroes but they were better than Manchester United and had several household names. As well as

George's Northern Ireland team mate Pat Jennings, they had the Welsh international centre half Mike England, who George had hoped would join him at Old Trafford.

Pat Jennings

They also boasted Alan Mullery, Joe Kinnear, Steve Perryman, Martin Chivers, Alan Gilzean and the World Cup winner Martin Peters. And at right

back they had that White Hart Lane icon Cyril Knowles, as in "Nice one Cyril". Tottenham would win the League Cup this season and finish third in the League.

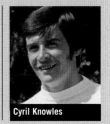
Cyril Knowles

Left: David Sadler (left) and Ian Ure.

Below: George (right) gets his head to the ball ahead of team mate Dave Sadler (centre) and Tottenham Hotspur's Mike England (left).

➤ died. On 4 January, George was up before the FA disciplinary committee for getting booked three times in twelve months. He had arranged to travel to London with Sir Matt for the hearing but missed the train and arrived three hours late. He was given a record £250 fine and a six-week suspended sentence. It was all over the papers.

On 8 January he missed another train: the one that was taking the team down to London to play Chelsea. In better times, he would have relished the prospect of a game at Stamford Bridge because he usually played well there, but such was his state of mind that it really didn't bother him not to go.

WEEKEND IN LONDON

He did, however, quite like the idea of a weekend in London and arranged to meet a female friend, the Irish actress Sinead Cusack. He spent the weekend with her at her flat in Islington, but the press got wind of it and when Sinead drew the curtains open on the Saturday morning she was confronted by a street full of reporters.

"What have you done, George?"

"Nothing," he replied. "I've just missed a football match, that's all."

👁 EYEWITNESS What the papers said...

"Isn't it time somebody told George Best he's getting far too big for his football boots? Or am I the only ex-fan who's sick of young twinkle ankles treating other people like they were the ball?" Jean Rook, The Daily Sketch

When he got back to Manchester the club suspended him for two weeks, during which time he played in a benefit game for the victims of Ibrox. And on 27 January he scored his only international hat trick as Northern Ireland beat Cyprus 5-0. Despite his mounting troubles George Best had proved he could still produce the goods, albeit not as often. *Sporting*LEGENDS

OFF THE PITCH **On this day**

A band called the Festfolk Quartet makes its debut performance in Gothenburg, Sweden. The group will later change its name to Abba.

THE RESULT

TOTTENHAM HOTSPUR	MANCHESTER UNITED	
2	**2**	**ATTENDANCE**
Gilzean, Peters	Best, Law	55,693

Right: George celebrates his opening goal.

Below: Denis Law scores Manchester United's second past Tottenham Hotspur goalkeeper Pat Jennings, as Mike England (left) and Martin Peters watch in vain.

© Colorsport

Sporting LEGENDS

GEORGE BEST MATCH PROGRAMME
1971-1972

Date **18 September 1971**
Venue **Old Trafford**
Kick-off **3pm**

MANCHESTER **UNITED** vs **WEST HAM**

FOOTBALL LEAGUE DIVISION ONE

Stepney

O'Neil

James

Sadler

Dunne

Gowling

Best

Morgan

Charlton

Law

Kidd

Best

Hurst

Robson

Brooking

Bonds

Redknapp

Moore

McDowell

Lampard

Taylor

Ferguson

LEAGUE DIVISION ONE

Manchester United
VS
West Ham United

VENUE	Old Trafford
DATE	Saturday, 18 September 1971
KICK-OFF	3pm

Manchester United were now routinely getting beaten by teams they used to destroy. Playing for a losing team had never been part of the plan, and it was something George didn't know how to handle – it was not something he had ever experienced. George was not enjoying his football. He had always been used to getting stick from opposition fans and that was never a problem, it meant they saw you as a threat, but by now the Old Trafford faithful were becoming ever more unhappy with the way their team was playing and had started booing their own players. So this hat trick was a ray of sunshine, and putting the great Bobby Moore on his backside for the third was the best part of it.

It was what they call a 'perfect' hat trick: one with the head, one with the left and one with the

Manchester United went into this game on the back of three straight wins. The previous Saturday they had beaten Crystal Palace 3-1 at Selhurst Park; the Wednesday before that they had won by the same scoreline in a League Cup match at Portman Road; and the Saturday before that they had beaten Ipswich 1-0 at Old Trafford in the League. They would not lose again until Leeds United came to Manchester on 30 October.

right. The first was the header, from a Bobby Charlton corner. The second was a beauty: "I cut in, beating several players following a short corner," George recalled. "I was off balance and remember trying to stop myself falling and hitting it with my weaker left foot and it flew into the net."

But it was the third that really made him feel proud. Coming over to collect another short corner, he goes past two players, including Bobby Moore, and hits it right-footed across Bobby Ferguson and into the net.

WARMEST MEMORIES

The way he fooled Bobby for that goal was, he said later, one of his "warmest memories" of the game. The year before Bobby had played in his second World Cup and had made *that* tackle on Pelé in the heat of Guadalajara. The England captain was universally recognised as one of the best defenders in the game, if not the best.

George certainly had a lot of respect for Bobby Moore. "The one thing I discovered over the ➤

> "*Not many strikers got one over on Bobby Moore. People always went on about his lack of speed but he didn't need pace because his timing in the tackle was immaculate and his reading of the game was so good.*" **George Best**

THE OPPOSITION

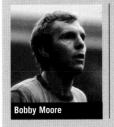
Bobby Moore

Clyde Best

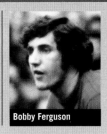
Bobby Ferguson

After the glory days of the mid-60s West Ham had slowly sunk to become a mid-table side. They had finished third from bottom of the League in 1970/71 and sixth from bottom the season before. This year they would improve slightly by finishing 14th but they were still three years away from winning another FA Cup. They remained, however, an entertaining side who would reach the semi finals of the League Cup this season before losing to Stoke City, and they still had Hurst and Moore.

Left: George Best looks happy again, and Bobby Moore (left) seems to be enjoying the moment with him.

Below: George takes on Billy Bonds (4) and Trevor Brooking.

DID YOU KNOW?

George would take the stick he got from opposition fans in good humour. At Anfield they used to sing "Georgie Best, Superstar, walks like a woman and he wears a bra" – so one day he borrowed a handbag from a tea lady just before kick-off and walked out onto the pitch carrying it under his arm.

years," he wrote in his autobiography *Blessed*, "was that he would rarely commit himself, leaving the striker to make all the difficult decisions. With other defenders I could drop a shoulder or feint to go to the right and they would dive in, leaving me the simple task of shifting to the left and getting my shot in." But this time Bobby did dive in and ended up sat helpless in the mud as George put the ball past Bobby Ferguson and into the corner of the net.

FRONT RUNNERS

This was Manchester United's ninth League game of the season and so far they had only lost one of those games, 1-0 at Goodison Park. Six wins and two draws had put them up amongst the front runners but it was early days and despite the good start there was no consistency in their results and they slipped to eighth place in the final table.

Manchester United were going nowhere. But George was. Instead of turning up to represent Northern Ireland in the Home Internationals at the end of the season as he was expected to, he got on an aeroplane and went to Marbella on holiday. There, less than a month after the end of the

Left to right: John McDowell, Tommy Taylor and Bobby Moore all stand to admire George's work.

1971/72 season, George Best would announce his retirement from football.

RASH DECISION

It was a rash decision, though it was one he had threatened to make before, but in his confusion it seemed like the right thing to do. He didn't know what he was going to do next but he felt pretty sure that he didn't want to play for Manchester United. He thought about signing for another club, but decided that he didn't want to play for anybody else. He had a vague idea about ➤

George shows off the extraordinary sense of balance that allowed him to change direction in a moment and fool defenders.

🕐 OFF THE PITCH
On this day
Seven-time Tour de France winner Lance Armstrong is born in Plano, Texas.

➤ following up his boutique business and becoming a fashion designer, but he knew that such a career wasn't ever going to fill the void that a life without football would create, and that he would always be living on his name in that business. But he needed to do something.

So what he did was he sat around the bars in Marbella waiting for someone from the club to come and try to persuade him to return to Manchester. But nobody came.

In the end, bored with the monotony, he went back of his own accord, tail between his legs, made his peace with Frank O'Farrell and began training, harder than ever, to get back into shape for the new season. *Sporting*LEGENDS

DID YOU KNOW?

George was sent off at Stamford Bridge in the second game of the 1971/72 season for fighting with team mate Willie Morgan. He admitted later on that he had actually been swearing at referee Norman Burtenshaw, so he kind of got away with that one.

This hat trick brought George's goal tally for the season to nine in all competitions – and the campaign was still only a month old.

THE RESULT

MANCHESTER UNITED	WEST HAM UNITED
4	**2**
Best (3), Charlton	Best, Brooking

ATTENDANCE 55,339

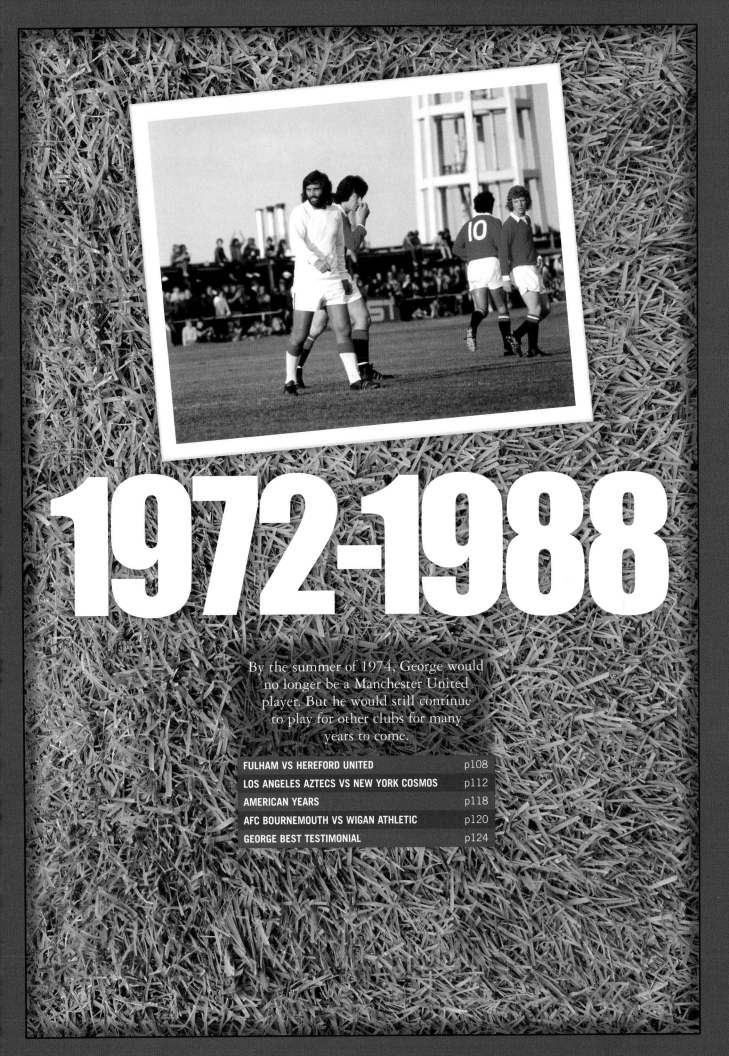

1972-1988

By the summer of 1974, George would no longer be a Manchester United player. But he would still continue to play for other clubs for many years to come.

Sporting LEGENDS **1976-1977**

George Best Match Programme

Fulham vs Hereford United

Date 25 September 1976 Venue Craven Cottage Kick-off 3pm

FOOTBALL LEAGUE DIVISION ONE

Mellor

Cutbush
Howe
Moore
Strong

Barrett
Slough
Evanson
Best

Mitchell
Marsh

Davey
McNeil

Spiring
Carter
Lindsay
Paine

Burrows
Galley
Layton
Tyler

Charlton

LEAGUE DIVISION TWO

Fulham

VS

Hereford United

VENUE	Craven Cottage
DATE	Saturday, 25 September 1976
KICK-OFF	3pm

Don't ever try to tell a Fulham supporter that George Best's career ended in 1974. Bobby Moore, George Best and Rodney Marsh were never going to get Fulham promoted back into the First Division – though for a while at the start of the 1976/77 season it looked like they might – but they did entertain and this game typifies the era.

The London Weekend Television cameras were there when Hereford United came to town, which was unusual for a Second Division game, and Best and Marsh used the opportunity to show off. There were cartwheels and American-style 'high fives'. It ended with the two of them tackling each other in the centre of the pitch, as a parody of how neither of the two ever had a reputation for being willing to pass the ball to a team mate. (George started it.) This was football as George had once enjoyed it, where entertainment came first and results just happened. "It's lovely to see kids leaning over the fence and laughing," was his abiding memory of those days at Craven Cottage.

Marsh scored twice against Hereford but there were other occasions when his tomfoolery didn't pay off, most notably when he once tried an ➤

The attendance for today's match at Craven Cottage was higher than the all-time record at Hereford's Edgar Road, which had stood at the 18,114 people who had turned up in January 1958 to watch United play Sheffield Wednesday in the third round of the FA Cup.

DID YOU KNOW?

When Barry Fry was making his managerial debut at Dunstable Town, the first thing he did was to ask George to do him a favour by turning out for the pre-season campaign. George never said no to a friend.

Old Trafford to Craven Cottage

AFTER LEAVING MANCHESTER UNITED, George became something of a one-man Harlem Globetrotters. In May 1974 he went to South Africa to play for the Jewish Guild and was next seen in Britain turning out for Dunstable Town that August in a pre-season friendly against Manchester United reserves. Dunstable had finished bottom of the League for eight years running and their last attendance had been 34. When George played the crowd was five figures.

Then, in November 1975 he was contracted for one month by Stockport County. Attendances at the Fourth Division club tripled, but it was never likely to last, especially as George was spending most of his spare time serving drinks and chat at his nightclub, Slack Alice. Still, in December 1975, it was reported that Chelsea were interested in signing him, but in the absence of any firm offer George signed to play for Los Angeles Aztecs for the 1976 season. While he was waiting for the summer to come round, he turned out for Cork Celtic in the Irish League but was dismissed after three matches for 'a lack of enthusiasm'.

George played that summer for the Aztecs and then, on 11 August 1976, he signed for Fulham. There he would join Bobby Moore, who had led the side out at Wembley in the 1975 FA Cup final against West Ham, and his old friend Rodney Marsh, who had just signed from Tampa Bay Rowdies.

THE OPPOSITION

Terry Paine

HEREFORD UNITED had won the Third Division Championship in 1976 and had got off to a good start in the Second Division, beating Hull City and Burnley and earning draws against Sheffield United and Carlisle.

They sat in ninth place going into this game, but the club that had famously knocked Newcastle United out of the FA Cup in 1972 would find themselves unable to cope with the demands of football at this level.

Dixie McNeill

After winning only six more League games all season, John Sillett's team, for whom the former Southampton star Terry Paine had postponed his retirement, finished bottom and went straight back down.

John Sillett

George slides in to block an attempted clearance from Hereford United's John Galley.

👁 EYEWITNESS **What the fans said...**

"George Best and Rodney Marsh cannot believe the space they are allowed to destroy United with a brilliant exhibition of trickery and cheek."

Ron Parrott, Hereford United - The League Era

anonymous, until he got himself sent off for arguing with the referee.

CALIFORNIA

The Southampton game was the start of a nine-game run without a win for Fulham, who ended the season narrowly avoiding relegation. In May, George flew out to America to play for Los Angeles Aztecs. He returned, due to contractual obligations, to play for Fulham again in 1977/78, but it was all over by Christmas. George returned to California and in January 1978 he married his first wife, Angie, whom he had met during his playing days in London. *Sporting*LEGENDS

➤ athletic bicycle kick and ended up putting the ball into his own net.

"What the hell were you trying to do out there?" asked the manager, Bedford Jezzard, whose job depended on results and not gate receipts.

"Entertain," said Rodney simply.

"If I wanted entertainment, son," replied Jezzard furiously, "I'd contact Billy Smart and sign two clowns."

"You've already got a first team full of them," said Marsh with his usual quick-fire wit. "Why do you want two more?"

ANONYMOUS

And that was the problem: Fulham weren't actually all that good. They'd started well but a week after this game they went to the Dell. The result of the match was the same: 4-1, but this time it was FA Cup holders Southampton who won comprehensively. George Best was largely

DID YOU KNOW?

In 1976, George also made a comeback as in international player, against the Netherlands in Rotterdam in a World Cup qualifier. The Irish, who had gone five games without a win, earned a 2-2 draw against Johan Cruyff's side.

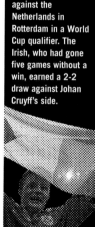

THE RESULT

FULHAM	HEREFORD UNITED
4	**1**
Slough, Evanson, Marsh (2)	Davey

ATTENDANCE
18,935

LEAGUE DIVISION TWO 1976/1977 FINAL TABLE

	P	W	D	L	F	A	PTS
17 Fulham	42	11	13	18	54	61	35
18 Cardiff City	42	12	10	20	56	67	34
19 Leyton Orient	42	9	16	17	37	55	34
20 Carlisle United	42	11	12	19	49	75	34
21 Plymouth Argyle	42	8	16	18	46	65	32
22 Hereford United	42	8	15	19	57	78	31

An inciteful look at the 50 best players competing in Germany this year. Discover the new stars before the tournament kicks off!

Sporting LEGENDS
GEORGE BEST MATCH PROGRAMME 1977

LOS ANGELES AZTECS
VS
NEW YORK COSMOS

Date 2 July 1977 Venue **Los Angeles Coliseum** Kick-off 2pm

NORTH AMERICAN SOCCER LEAGUE

Rigby

Beal   McGrane

Sibbald   Mancini   Best

McAlinden

Cohen   Cooke   David

Davies

Pelé   Chinaglia

Garbett   Field

Hunt   Mifflin   Morais

Roth

Rildo   Dillon

Messing

Los Angeles Aztecs
VS
New York Cosmos

VENUE	Los Angeles Coliseum
DATE	Saturday, 2 July 1977
KICK-OFF	2pm

Part-owner Elton John with George and the Aztecs at the Los Angeles Coliseum.

The reaction of the Aztecs fans to Franz Beckenbauer's absence from the Cosmos line-up demonstrates well the vast difference between British football culture and that of North America in the 1970s. While British fans would have been pleased to see that the opposition's star player was out injured, the fans in the Los Angeles Coliseum jeered the news. They had come to see a show and without Beckenbauer, who they suspected wasn't really injured anyway, they were not getting their full money's worth.

But what they would witness was Pelé's last ever game in competitive football. And, whether they fully appreciated it or not, it is fitting that the architect of the Cosmos' defeat today was the man Pelé himself considered to have been the world's greatest ever player: George Best.

➤

" It was our best game this year. The way we played today, I don't think Beckenbauer could have made any difference. We knew we had to take it to them and that's exactly what we did. " **George Best**

THE OPPOSITION

Pelé

Ghinaglia

THE NEW YORK COSMOS were the biggest club in the North American Soccer League and, with their large European and South American immigrant fanbase, they were also one of its biggest draws in terms of both attendances and TV audiences. On this day they were without their captain Franz Beckenbauer, who had joined them from Bayern Munich as the current European Footballer of the Year. But beyond their mongrel assortment of young American hopefuls and ageing British journeymen, they also had the former Italian international Giorgio Chinaglia, as well as the Brazilian full backs Nelsi Morais and Rildo – and, of course, their compatriot, Pelé.

➤ INTERNAL SQUABBLING

Although Pelé's contributions over the season would help the Cosmos to the 1977 NASL Championships, this was not the end to an illustrious career the great man might have hoped for. Having joined the Cosmos in 1975, at the age of 35, Pelé had since become increasingly disenchanted with the way the team was not being built around him, as he felt he had been led to believe it would be.

A feud seems to have developed between himself and the team's other main star, the Italian striker Giorgio Chinaglia. This feud was allowed to spread to the pitch. The Brazilians passed to Pelé and not Chinaglia; the Brits passed to Chinaglia but that usually meant long, high balls down the middle, which is not what the Italian had been brought up on in his seven years of calcio in Serie A.

The result was that New York fans never saw the best of either player. This Cosmos side became notorious throughout the NASL for its internal squabbling and when they were outplayed, as they were today, they were beatable. ➤

Left: George Best, dribbles past Pelé.

Right: Eddie Firmani, Head coach of the New York Cosmos.

DID YOU KNOW?
Despite the lack of harmony in the dressing room, this Cosmos team would eventually win the NASL Championships, not only this season but also in 1978, 1980 and 1982.

OFF THE PITCH Number 1
2 July 1977

🇬🇧 Hot Chocolate **So You Win Again**

🇺🇸 Bill Conti **Gonna Fly Now (Theme from *Rocky*)**

© Colorsport

© Colorsport

Despite losing their last two Southern Division games after this win, the Aztecs went on to make it as far as the 1977 Conference Championships, where they lost to the Seattle Sounders.

proud of that moment too: "Seeing the Cosmos defenders go with David," George explained, "I changed direction left, took the ball round Pelé, and found myself flat on the ground, professionally fouled by the greatest player the game has known. I should have been angry, but in a funny way I took it as a compliment."

George's 18 'assists' for the Aztecs over the 1977 season equalled Pelé's all-time NASL record – and he might have beaten it too, if it hadn't been for that meddling Brazilian.

But Pelé wasn't there to foul Best the second time, when George saw Charlie Cooke set off looking for a similar 'wide receiver' pass with the score already at 3-1 to the Californians. George found his team mate with pinpoint precision and then Cooke crossed the ball perfectly for Steve David to rush in and head home his second of the game and his team's fourth. *Sporting*LEGENDS

➤ The first goal came from a Phil Beal penalty, after the Aztecs' Trinidadian striker Steve David had been fouled by Rildo in the box. David then made it 2-0 after making the most of a deft pass from George Best. The Cosmos pulled one back from the penalty spot through their own principal marksman, but then Terry Mancini restored the Aztecs' advantage after a free kick was awarded for obstruction on Best.

RAKING PASSES
But the fourth goal was the finest of them all. George was becoming known for his long, raking passes from midfield and earlier in the game, while he was threatening one such delivery towards Steve David, he had found himself on the end of a professional foul by Pelé – he was quite

DID YOU KNOW?
The North American Soccer League was founded in 1968 when the United Soccer Association and the National Professional Soccer League converged.

THE RESULT

LOS ANGELES AZTECS	NEW YORK COSMOS
4	**1**
Beal (pen), David (2), Mancini	Chinaglia (pen)

ATTENDANCE 32,165

AMERICAN YEARS

" I got the ball 25 yards from goal and sidestepped the defender. There were three more waiting to pick me off but I dummied them left, then right, then left again and shook them all off and as the keeper came out I knocked it past him." **George Best**

With their galaxies of European and South American stars – and large immigrant populations from these continents – teams like the Los Angeles Aztecs, the Tampa Bay Rowdies and the New York Cosmos could draw sizeable crowds. But over the United States as a whole, soccer in the 1970s was by no means a big spectator sport.

This had its advantages. For one thing, it meant that, for the first time in well over a decade, George could go to the shops without fear of being molested by fans, or worse, punched in the face for 'throwing it all away'.

For another, it meant escape from the heavy drinking culture that was endemic in the British game. George claimed that when he first arrived in California, he hardly drank at all – maybe a bottle of beer after training, but nothing more. He was happy just to go jogging along the beach, enjoy the sunshine, and play a few games of none-too-taxing football.

BOBBY MAC

His old friend Bobby McAlinden, the former Manchester City youth team player, who had gone to California with him – at George's behest and expense – would make sure he got his friend down onto the beach at Hermosa every morning,

Right: George challenges New York's Keith Eddy for the ball.

"working off the effects of four years' heavy drinking and that crazy upside-down life I'd led since opening Slack Alice."

George was now dividing his time between Los Angeles and London. He played the 1976 NASL season for the Los Angeles Aztecs, returned to Fulham for the 1976/77 season, played the 1977 season for the Aztecs, and then went back to London again for the 1977/78 Second Division season. By November, however, he had been suspended by the London club for not turning up for training. The reason: he had already returned to Los Angeles.

In June 1978 he was traded to the Fort Lauderdale Strikers, but as far as Fulham were concerned he was still their player. On 11 October he was banned by FIFA from playing for anybody until the contract dispute with Fulham was resolved. The following day his mother was found dead at home in Belfast; it was her drinking that killed her. Ann Best was 54. She had been teetotal until the age of 40.

REFUSED TESTIMONIAL

George was permitted to return to Florida for the 1979 season but was soon suspended by the Strikers for 'going missing'. He was refused a

testimonial by Manchester United in October and signed for Hibernian in November. Again, it didn't last long. After being suspended by his club again for failing to be fit for a Scottish Cup match in February 1980, he admitted that he had a 'drink problem'.

SAN JOSÉ EARTHQUAKES

George returned once again to the United States to play for the San José Earthquakes in the 1980 season, and in 1981 he scored one of his greatest ever goals for them, ducking and darting right and left, past several defenders before beating the keeper from within the six-yard box.

It wasn't on the biggest stage but it was a quite magnificent goal. George had proved to the world that he could still do it. He just couldn't do it very often. *Sporting*LEGENDS

Los Angeles Aztecs' George Best (centre) mesmerizes several New York Cosmos players with his ball skills.

Sporting LEGENDS

GEORGE BEST
MATCH PROGRAMME
1982-1983
AFC Bournemoth vs Wigan Athletic
Date 7 May 1983
Venue Dean Court
Kick-off **3pm**

AFC

BOURNEMOUTH

FOOTBALL LEAGUE DIVISION ONE

Leigh

Heffernan   Brignull   Impey   Sulley

Best   Shaw   Spackman   Nightingale

Morgan   Lee

O'Keefe

Houghton   Langley   Sheldon

Young   Weston   Butler

Lowe   Methven   Cribley

Tunks

❧ LEAGUE DIVISION THREE ❧
AFC Bournemouth
VS
Wigan Athletic

VENUE	Dean Court
DATE	Saturday, 7 May 1983
KICK-OFF	3pm

Bournemouth had first expressed an interest in George as long ago as December 1972, though at that time they had little chance of signing him, especially with clubs like Chelsea in the hunt for the transfer-listed striker. But this time Brian Tiler had gone to some considerable effort to persuade George to play for his club, eventually tracking him down to a bar in London.

George didn't really want to play for Bournemouth, despite the fact that he would only be expected to turn up on a Saturday whenever there was a home game: "It was the usual thing: they wanted me just for home games, to put a few on the gate." But neither did he want to say no to somebody he liked and respected. So he did his usual disappearing act. He told Brian to get some champagne in to celebrate the deal, excused himself to go to the lavatory and sneaked out of the window and off to a bar he thought nobody knew he frequented. But Tiler found him. And so George pulled the same trick again.

STRONG RUMOURS
In September 1981 George had played for a

> These two teams were heading in opposite directions: Bournemouth's future looked promising; Wigan were in deep financial trouble.

> **DID YOU KNOW?**
> When George played for Bournemouth against Southend United at Roots Hall on 16 April 1983, 4,275 people turned up to watch.

Middlesbrough select XI in Jim Platt's testimonial. This had led to strong rumours that he was going to return to England and resume his career at Ayresome Park, but despite an announcement from the club in December that they had signed him, it did not happen.

George quickly quelled the speculation by telling the press that he would not be playing for Middlesbrough Football Club.

BANKRUPT
Instead, after being declared bankrupt in 1982, he signed for Bournemouth on 24 March 1983 and made his debut for the Cherries against Newport County two days later – 9,121 people packed Dean Court for the occasion. In all he made five appearances for the club, of which this was the last – and indeed his last appearance in an ➤

👁 EYEWITNESS What the players said...

"I saw George at Dean Court when Bournemouth played Newport County, and he cut a sorry, almost pathetic figure, going through the motions in journeyman company." **Joe Lovejoy**

THE OPPOSITION

Kevin Langley

Colin Methven

WIGAN ATHLETIC might be flying high in the English Premiership this season but in May 1983 they were in dire straits. Chairman Freddie Pye had been close to putting the club into liquidation before chief shareholder Ken Bates (the very same) stepped in. And their prospects were not looking any rosier on the pitch. Having been promoted from the Football League basement the previous season, the Latics now sat just above the drop zone and an immediate return to the Fourth Division looked more than possible. In desperation, they had just sacked their manager Larry Lloyd (the former Liverpool and Nottingham Forest centre back) and a certain Bobby Charlton had taken over as caretaker for the visit to Dean Court. He would only be there for one match, but it was this one.

OFF THE PITCH Number 1
7 May 1983

🇬🇧	Spandau Ballet **True**
🇺🇸	Michael Jackson **Beat It**

➤ English League match. He was two weeks short of his 37th birthday and now a father to two-year-old Calum.

GREAT POTENTIAL

George was described in the match programme as 'portly' – the years of heavy drinking had had a noticeable effect on his physical appearance – though he could have scored with a thunderous shot that rattled the crossbar. But it was a Mark Nightingale header that put the home side in front and their lead was doubled just before the break by top scorer Trevor Morgan, but Wigan came back with two goals in the second half to earn the point they so desperately needed.

Bournemouth were clear of relegation and had just had another bumper gate. They were also a team on the up. In his post-match interview, George told reporters: "There is obviously great potential at this club. With a little bit of strengthening in the squad they must have a good chance of making a promotion place next season."

George cuts a 'portly' figure at Dean Court.

👁 EYEWITNESS What the papers said...

"GEORGE GIVES THUMBS UP TO THE CHERRIES"

Bournemouth Evening Echo

DID YOU KNOW?
On 7 January 1984, AFC Bournemouth beat Manchester United 2-0 in the third round of the FA Cup.

Under Harry Redknapp, who took over as manager from Don Megson that summer, the Cherries did indeed win promotion, though not until 1987. George went from Bournemouth to Australia, where in July 1983 he played four games for Brisbane Lions of Queensland and one game for Osborne Park Galeb of Western Australia. His last ever competitive match was for Tobermore United against Ballymena United in the Irish Cup in January 1984. *Sporting*LEGENDS

THE RESULT		
AFC BOURNEMOUTH	**WIGAN ATHLETIC**	
2	**2**	ATTENDANCE
Nightingale, Morgan	Lowe, Houghton	4,523

For the best coverage of Italian football in the UK read Calcio Italia – the in-depth monthly magazine for lovers of the beautiful game played in the country of passion.

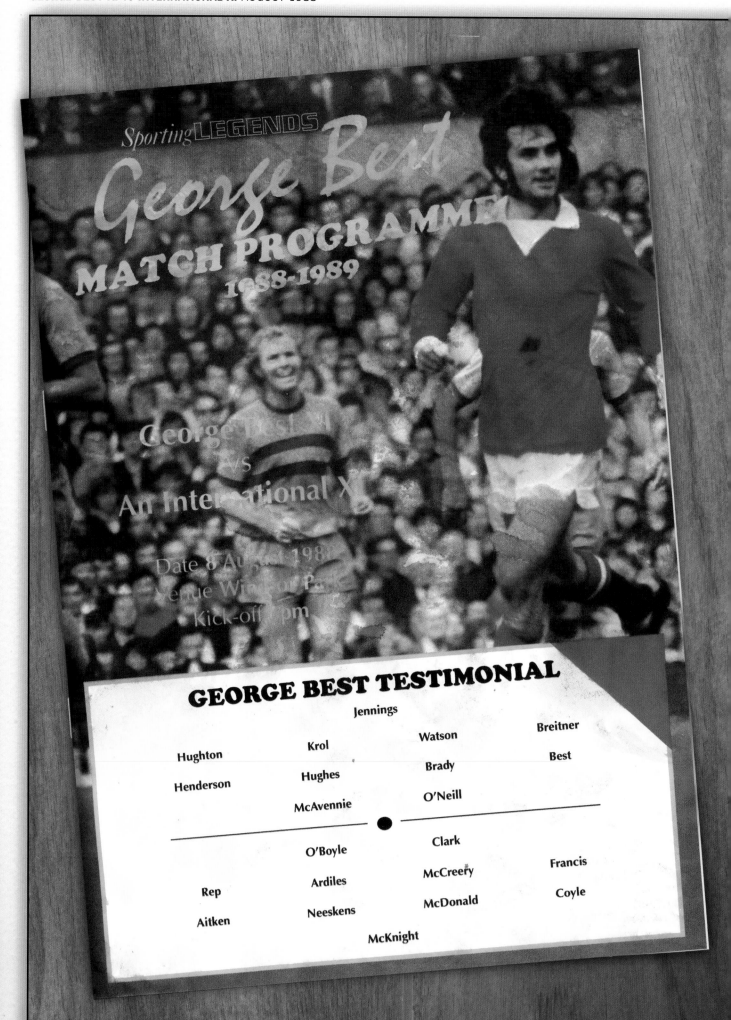

Sporting **LEGENDS**

George Best

MATCH PROGRAMME
1988-1989

George Best XI
vs
An International XI

Date 8 August 1988
Venue Windsor Park
Kick-off 7pm

GEORGE BEST TESTIMONIAL

Jennings

Watson · Breitner

Hughton · Krol

Brady · Best

Henderson · Hughes

O'Neill

McAvennie

Clark

O'Boyle

McCreery · Francis

Rep · Ardiles

McDonald · Coyle

Aitken · Neeskens

McKnight

George Best XI
VS
International XI

VENUE	Windsor Park
DATE	Monday, 8 August 1988
KICK-OFF	8pm

There were a number of people who thought this match should never have gone ahead. Indeed, six months earlier the Irish Football Association had refused George's initial request for a testimonial. The television pundit and former Liverpool player Ian St John summed up the mood of the dissenters: "Testimonials are usually for players who have really put something into the game," he argued. "It's a thank you. And you couldn't say that George really put an awful lot into the game for his country or for his clubs, because he packed it in when he was 27 years old." But not everybody thought like St John and George's supporters were numerous and vociferous enough to persuade the IFA to reverse its earlier decision.

Among the players starting on the bench for the two squads were Allan Clarke, John Collins, Andy Gray, Mark Lawrenson, Sammy McIlroy, Wolfgang Overath, Peter Reid, John Robertson, Kenny Samson and Frank Stapleton.

"The original committee were only asking for permission," explained George. "That's all they wanted and then they were going to do all the hard work." Never the less, Belfast's most famous son had all but given up hope of a match in his honour by the time he heard that permission would be granted after all: "I really am very pleasantly surprised," he kept saying. "I thought it was a lost cause."

FOOTBALL PARTY
But the doubts that his initial rejection had caused were still there. Three months before the game, as arrangements were being made, he seemed unsure of the support he would get on the night. He was throwing a football party in his home town and he wasn't sure if anybody would come. But he was philosophical about it: "It's up to the general public," he shrugged. "If nobody shows up then that's up to them, and if it's full on the night then that's also up to them. It's ➤

> *"George is a man who very rarely says no to people. He's played in 150 testimonials that I can think of. He's never said no to anybody who needed him and I don't think the Irish people should say no when he needs them."* **Angie Best**

THE OPPOSITION

IT WAS AN ILLUSTRIOUS twenty-two who made the effort to come to Belfast for the game. Germany's World Cup hero Paul Breitner was joined by the Dutch stars Rudi Krol, Johan

Neeskens and Johnny Rep. The Celtic and Scotland captain Roy Aitken and his compatriot Frank McAvennie were there, along with England's Dave Watson, Emlyn Hughes and Trevor Francis. Pat

Jennings returned the compliment George had paid him two years earlier, while Alan McKnight, Alan McDonald, Colin Clark and David McCreery represented Northern Ireland on

Johnny Rep

the International XI, and the Republic's Chris Hughton and Liam Brady played for George's team. Ossie Ardiles played and there was also room for young Darren Coyle and George O'Boyle from Linfield.

Emlyn Hughes

➤ they who decide. If someone thinks I don't deserve it they don't have to come."

But they did come, and from all corners of the globe. When George finally trotted out into the rainy night, heavily bearded and with his son Calum by his side, he was met with the applause of the biggest crowd Windsor Park had seen since the Pat Jennings testimonial in December 1986.

FIRST TOUCH

George's first touch isn't a particularly good one. Liam Brady sprays the ball out to him on the left touchline and it slips on the greasy surface under his foot and into touch. But as the game goes on he starts to settle down and enjoy himself, and in a game of thirteen goals, his first was probably the best of the lot – a sublime right-footed chip from just outside the area. (Though having said that, Liam Brady's left-footed second was something pretty special too, and even Bill McMurdo, George's long-time agent, came on as a substitute to bag a fair effort for himself.)

George's own second goal came from the penalty spot. The game was delicately poised at 6-6 and it was perhaps a generous decision by the referee, but nobody was complaining that hard

Below: George's team for the night. Hughes, Breitner, Watson, Krol, O'Neill; Hughton, McAvennie, Jennings, Best, Brady and Henderson.

DID YOU KNOW?
Angie might only have remembered 150 of them but George himself claimed to have played in "three to four hundred" testimonials by the time his own was staged.

and although he never took the set pieces for Manchester United, tonight it was always going to be the man in the number 11 shirt who took the kick that decided the game.

"Phenomenal," was George's verdict on the night, his face beaming with happiness. "The crowd was fabulous. It's pouring down with rain and they're standing there like they don't have a care in the world." *Sporting*LEGENDS

THE RESULT

ATTENDANCE 30,000	GEORGE BEST XI	INTERNATIONAL XI
	Brady (2), McAvennie, Breitner, McCoy, Best (2, 1 pen) **7**	**6** McDonald, Francis (2), O'Boyle, Clark, McMurdo

CAREER RECORD

"He had everything. He had the skill, he was brave, he was good in the air, he scored goals, he never stopped running. He was a magnificent player." **Denis Law**

A Appearances
G Goals

CAREER STATISTICS											
Manchester United May 1963-January 1974											
Season	League		FA Cup		League Cup		European Cup		ECWC		Fairs/UEFA Cup	
	A	G	A	G	A	G	A	G	A	G	A	G
1963/64	17	4	7	2					2	0		
1964/65	41	10	7	2							11	2
1965/66	31	9	5	3			6	4				
1966/67	42	10	2	0	1	0						
1967/68	41	28	2	1			9	3				
1968/69	41	19	6	1			6	2				
1969/70	37	15	7	6	8	2						
1970/71	40	18	2	1	6	2						
1971/72	40	18	7	7	6	3						
1972/73	19	4			4	2						
1973/74	12	2										
Total	361	137	45	23	25	9	21	9	2	0	11	2

TOTALS	A	G
League	361	137
Domestic cups	70	32
European club	34	11
Overall	465	180

INTERNATIONAL	
Northern Ireland	
Caps	37
Goals	9

George shows his 1967-68 Footballer of the Year award to Sir Matt Busby.

George in action for Manchester United against Manchester City in September 1967.

> *" I've got my memories, they're all great, they're all good memories and nobody had a friend as good as George Best to me."* **Bobby McAlinden**

	League		FA Cup		League Cup	
	A	**G**	**A**	**G**	**A**	**G**
Jewish Guild May 1974-June 1974						
1974	5	not known				
Stockport County November 1975-December 1975						
1975/76	3	2				
Cork Celtic December 1975-January 1976						
1975/76	3	0				
Los Angeles Aztecs April 1976-August 1976						
1976	24	15				
Fulham September 1976-May 1977						
1976/77	32	6	2	0	3	2
Los Angeles Aztecs May 1977-August 1977						
1977	25	13				
Fulham September 1977-November 1977						
1977/78	10	2				
Los Angeles Aztecs April 1978-June 1978						
1978	12	1				
Fort Lauderdale Strikers June 1978-July 1979						
1978/79	33	7				
Hibernian November 1979-April 1980						
1979/80	13	3	3	0		
San José Earthquakes April 1980-August 1980						
1980	26	8				
Hibernian September 1980-October 1980						
1980/81	4	0				
San José Earthquakes March 1981-August 1981						
1981	30	13				
AFC Bournemouth March 1983-May 1983						
1982/83	5	0				
Brisbane Lions						
1983	4	0				
Ballymena United						
1983/84			1	0		

George Best with a football, a pressman and a policeman. Quite appropriately.

*Sporting*LEGENDS

GEORGE BEST
HIS GREATEST MATCHES

ACKNOWLEDGEMENTS

Best: An Intimate Biography Michael Parkinson
The Best of Times George Best, Les Scott
Bestie Joe Lovejoy
Blessed George Best
Denis Law: An Autobiography Denis Law
George and Me Angie Best
George Best: Tribute to a Legend David Meek
George Best and 21 Others Colin Shindler
George Best Soccer Annuals 1968-1972 Pelham Books
The Good, the Bad and the Bubbly George Best and Ross Benson
Hamlyn Illustrated History of Manchester United
Hard Tackles and Dirty Baths George Best
Hereford United: the League Era Ron Parrott
The King Denis Law, Bob Harris
McIlvanney on Football Hugh McIlvanney
Scoring at Half Time George Best
Sir Matt Busby: A Tribute Rick Glanvill
A Strange Kind of Glory Eamon Dunphy
Where Do I Go From Here? George Best, Angela Janes, Graeme Wright

NEWSPAPERS
The Bournemouth Evening Echo
The Daily Express
The Daily Mail
The Daily Mirror
The Guardian
The Independent
The Los Angeles Times
The Manchester Evening News
The Observer

VIDEOS/DVDS
Best Best Films Ltd
George Best: Genius. The Official Video Autobiography CBS/Fox Video Ltd
The George Best Story Ulster Television
The Official George Best Story Video Collection International Ltd

WEBSITES
www.11v11.co.uk
www.manutd.com
www.red11.org
www.redissue.co.uk
www.shankly.com
www.stretfordend.co.uk

MANY THANKS
Mark Baber, Association of Football Statisticians
Ivan Ponting

INDEX